# cook what you love

# cook what you love

SIMPLE, FLAVORFUL RECIPES TO MAKE AGAIN AND AGAIN

Bob and Melinda Blanchard

Photographs by Ellen Silverman

Clarkson Potter/Publishers
New York

Published by Clarkson Potter/Publishers, an imprint of the Crown Publishing Group,
a division of Random House, Inc., New York.
www.clarksonpotter.com



Library of Congress Cataloging-in-Publication Data
Blanchard, Robert, 1951–
Cook what you love / Bob and Melinda Blanchard ; photographs by
Ellen Silverman.—1st ed.
Includes index.
1. Cookery. I. Blanchard, Melinda, 1952– II. Title.
TX714.B574823 2005
641.5—dc22 2004029002

ISBN 1-4000-5439-7

Printed in Singapore

Design by Maggie Hinders with Lisa Sloane

10 9 8 7 6 5 4 3 2 1

First Edition

# Contents

# Cook What You Love

The debate about whether to write another cookbook continued for many months in our house. Certainly, everyone has access to enough recipes with thousands of volumes already published, not to mention scores of Web sites guiding you through every cuisine imaginable. But if our bookshelves are any indication, people buy cookbooks for less obvious reasons than collecting recipes.

Food historian Barbara Haber says, "Like other good books, the best cookbooks have strong voices that lure readers into unfamiliar worlds, give colorful observations about those places, and, above all, reveal a passionate interest in sharing pleasure. . . . Why cookbooks offer such gratification is usually explained by pointing out the benefits of living vicariously—reading about rich foods instead of eating them, or learning about the cuisine and culture of Southern India without investing in an expensive trip."

It turns out that Barbara's words ring true for many people and that, indeed, there's plenty of room for another cookbook—as long as it has some soul. Our first book, *A Trip to the Beach,* tells the story of how we moved to the tiny Caribbean island of Anguilla to open a restaurant. To our surprise, that little book turned out to be an inspiration for tens of thousands of people. We certainly never expected to receive daily e-mails from readers who wanted to hear more of our stories.

Our first cookbook, *At Blanchard's Table,* is filled with recipes from both our worlds, Vermont and Anguilla. What readers comment on time and time again are the stories between the recipes: stories about people, food, and how they interact. That's how we came to write this second cookbook. Cooking what we love is about food, people, and celebrating the pleasure that comes from bringing them together. It is about why we cook rather than what we cook.

It's taken us a while to realize exactly why we feel the way we do about food. It's the sharing of honest and often delicious experiences with anyone, anywhere. The language we speak doesn't matter, nor does the color of our skin, our age, or our political and religious beliefs. Food is something we have in common with every other person in the world. That's a reason to celebrate.

We've always believed in following our dreams and passions, in living out what we truly love. For us, that philosophy has more than once led us into the food world. Living what you love, however, doesn't have to mean opening a restaurant or starting a specialty food business. It can be as simple as spending more time with your family and friends, appreciating life's little pleasures. While enjoying these moments, we've often found that food is somehow a part of the experience, from celebration dinners to picnics on the beach to breakfast in bed.

This book combines nearly a hundred of our favorite recipes with stories about how our love for food seeps into every part of life. The pleasure we get from discovering a new roadside café, starting an herb garden, or gathering friends around a campfire is all part of the fun. Our hope is to bring friends, family, and sometimes even strangers together to create great memories in the kitchen and around the table.

With everyone's busy lives in mind, the recipes here are quick and simple. The ingredients are readily available, and we've included prep time and cooking time to help you plan each meal. We are honored to share our recipes and stories with you and hope you enjoy many wonderful meals together.

# Prep Like the Pros

When people ask us for cooking tips, our first response is always the same: "Get organized before you start." Call it prep work, *mise-en-place,* or whatever you like, but the key to success with recipes in any cookbook is to follow these three easy steps.

1. Before you begin, read the entire recipe from start to finish.

2. Place all of the ingredients on the kitchen counter.

3. Prepare and measure each ingredient* and line them up on the counter in the same order they're called for in the recipe. This step includes chopping, slicing, trimming, and anything that needs to be done before the actual cooking begins.

If everything is lined up and ready to go in advance, all you have to do is assemble the ingredients according to the recipe. Whether you're sautéing, baking, grilling, or roasting, with everything organized before you start to cook, the entire process becomes more enjoyable. There's no running back to the refrigerator searching for a missing clove of garlic or rushing to chop some herbs at the last minute.

*Treat yourself to a few extra sets of measuring cups and small bowls to help organize your ingredients before you start to cook. Many kitchenware stores sell wonderful little sets of glass prep bowls that you will find indispensable.

# A Few Details Make the Difference

Here are some basic ingredients we always have on hand. We've listed brand names only when we feel they are superior and significantly affect the quality of the final dish.

### BREAD CRUMBS

Japanese bread crumbs (called Panko) are available in the Asian aisle of most supermarkets these days. The usual American variety often becomes mushy instead of crispy when cooked. We prefer Panko because it adds more crunch and wonderful texture to any recipe calling for a bread-crumb topping.

### BUTTER

We use only unsalted butter. The salted variety forces you to add more salt than you may want in a recipe, and it's impossible to counteract that effect. Unsalted butter allows you to have much more control.

### CHOCOLATE WAFERS

Several of our recipes call for Nabisco Famous Chocolate Wafers. These are readily available in many parts of the country, but we've discovered that for some reason they are just not distributed in certain regions. If you have trouble finding them, substitute another plain chocolate cookie. If the recipe calls for cookie crumbs, Oreos work surprisingly well. When you crush an Oreo, the creamy filling magically disappears and you're left with perfect chocolate crumbs.

### CHICKEN BROTH

If you haven't discovered boxes of chicken broth in the soup aisle of your grocery store, we urge you to buy some right away. It's as close to homemade as you can get, without any effort whatsoever. And, as an extra bonus, it comes with a recloseable spout so you can use as much or as little as you want at one time.

### LEMON JUICE

We use a lot of freshly squeezed lemon juice, and you'll see it called for frequently throughout the book. If you buy a wooden citrus reamer, it makes the task quite painless. But if time is tight, Minute Maid sells 100% pure frozen lemon juice that's an excellent substitute. This is entirely different from the artificial version found in the produce department, which doesn't taste like real lemon juice at all.

### LIME JUICE

Unfortunately, there is no good substitute for freshly squeezed lime juice. Luckily, none of our recipes call for very much of it, so it's worth the effort.

### PARMESAN CHEESE

We love Parmesan cheese! Though you can buy it already grated, we usually buy whole chunks and grate it ourselves. When we can, we use Parmigiano-Reggiano. It hails from Parma, Italy, and has the perfect combination of flavor and texture. It's more expensive than others, but we think it's well worth it. However, don't worry—there are acceptable substitutes available in grocery stores across the country. And by all means, forget the cans of powdered cheese sold near the pasta section. It doesn't even come close to the real thing!

### SALT

If you don't keep a small bowl of kosher salt near the stove, we urge you to give it a try. Once you start pinching instead of shaking, you'll never go back.

# Breakfast

* Crunchy Coconut French Toast
* Orange-Currant Muffins
* One-Eyed Jacks
* Spanish Scrambled Eggs
* Scrambled Eggs with Pepper Boursin
* Sweet Basil Bacon
* Strawberry Butter
* Cinnamon-Maple Butter
* Cranberry Coffee Cake

# breakfast in bed

What do you do when your wife is a chef and you want to make her a special meal? I have asked myself this question many times over the past thirty years. What I finally figured out is that it's not the complexity of the food but the experience of sharing it that matters most. Breakfast in bed is one of life's ultimate and simplest indulgences. It's comfort food in a very comfortable place. Often overlooked, it can be more romantic than a candlelit dinner at a five-star restaurant.

Melinda is an early riser. A *real* early riser. She loves describing the sunrise she sees from her office each

morning. I, on the other hand, start my day at a much more civilized hour. But several years ago, Mel was up late one night and slept until almost 9:00. (Imagine!) For some reason, I was up early and decided to take advantage of the opportunity. This was my chance to be romantic and spontaneous. I had no doubt that combining food with a little spontaneity would make her smile—which is really what our relationship is all about. We love to make each other smile.

I searched through cookbooks for breakfast ideas using ingredients we already had in the house, resulting in my own version of recipes that now appear in this book. That first breakfast in bed was quite elaborate (for me, anyway): Scrambled Eggs with Pepper Boursin, Sweet Basil Bacon, Orange-Currant Muffins served warm with Strawberry Butter. It took three trays to get it all upstairs but it sure was a hit.

Since then, I have to admit, I sometimes just bring a simple bowl of cereal and some coffee or just toast with the morning paper, but I'm always greeted with a smile. If I hear Mel padding around upstairs once I've started cooking, I'll tell her to get back into bed. She never refuses and always loves the surprise.

So go ahead. Be romantic. Treat someone you love like royalty. Even if it's just once a year, it will become a ritual worth repeating.

# Crunchy Coconut French Toast

French toast is one of our favorite breakfast dishes, so we've experimented with many variations of the classic recipe. We served brunch for a brief time at our restaurant, and this was one of the most popular dishes on the menu. The sweet coconut gives it a Caribbean flavor, while the maple syrup conjures up thoughts of our home in Vermont.

PREP TIME: 7 MINUTES
COOKING TIME: 5 MINUTES
SERVES 4

1 1/4 cups shredded unsweetened coconut (see Note)
3 cups cornflakes, slightly crushed
4 large eggs
1/4 cup milk
1 teaspoon pure vanilla extract
4 (1-inch-thick) slices challah or 4 croissants, sliced lengthwise
1 tablespoon unsalted butter
Real Vermont maple syrup, for serving

Place the coconut and cornflakes in a shallow bowl and mix well.

In another shallow bowl, lightly whisk together the eggs, milk, and vanilla. Dip the bread slices into the egg mixture and soak for about a minute on each side. They should be well coated but not soggy. Press each slice into the coconut mixture on both sides, patting firmly and turning them over several times to coat thoroughly.

Heat the butter on a griddle or in a large sauté pan over medium heat. Cook for 2 to 3 minutes on each side, or until golden brown and cooked through. Serve with warm maple syrup.

**NOTE:** It's important to use unsweetened coconut in this recipe. The sweetened variety is too moist and makes the bread soggy.

# Orange-Currant Muffins

These muffins are a delicious way to surprise your loved one with breakfast in bed on a rainy Sunday morning, as Bob has done for years. Serve them hot out of the oven with the Strawberry Butter on page 24.

PREP TIME: 12 MINUTES
COOKING TIME: 25 TO 30 MINUTES
MAKES 12 MUFFINS

2½ cups all-purpose flour
¼ cup sugar
1½ tablespoons baking powder
¼ teaspoon kosher salt
½ teaspoon grated fresh orange peel (see Note)
½ cup (1 stick) unsalted butter, at room temperature
1 cup cold milk
1 cup dried currants

Preheat the oven to 350°F. Line a muffin tin with 12 paper inserts or grease well with butter.

In a large bowl, whisk together the flour, sugar, baking powder, and salt. Add the orange peel and mix well. Using your hands or a pastry blender, work the butter into the flour mixture until it resembles coarse meal. Gradually stir in the milk and currants, mixing as little as possible just until the flour is moist.

Spoon the batter into the 12 muffin cups and bake for 25 minutes or until golden brown. Serve warm.

**NOTE:** When grating the orange peel, be careful to grate only the outer layer, avoiding the bitter white pith underneath.

# One-Eyed Jacks

We love traveling and discovering different names for foods we've known our whole lives. This childhood favorite has countless names, depending on where you're from: egg-in-the-hole, bull's-eye, and picture-frame egg, to name a few. No matter what you call it, this simple breakfast is sure to bring smiles to your table. We love them as much now as we did when we were kids.

PREP TIME: 2 MINUTES
COOKING TIME: 5 MINUTES
SERVES 2

4 slices good-quality sandwich bread
3 tablespoons unsalted butter
4 large eggs
Kosher salt and freshly ground black pepper

Cut a 2-inch hole in the center of each slice of bread. You can use a biscuit cutter if one is handy, but a knife works just fine.

In a large sauté pan, heat the butter over medium-high heat until the foaming subsides. Arrange the bread slices in the pan and cook until golden brown on one side, about 2 minutes. Turn the bread over and crack an egg into the center of each. Sprinkle with salt and pepper and cook for 1 minute. Reduce the heat to low, and cook the eggs to desired doneness, turning again if you like.

# Spanish Scrambled Eggs

We're always looking for ways to add color and texture to a recipe. Food seems to taste better if it looks beautiful. Roasted whole cherry tomatoes are a quick, easy way to brighten up a platter of these or any other scrambled eggs. Just toss the tomatoes with a little olive oil, salt, and pepper and roast at 400°F for about 10 minutes, or until hot and wrinkled. Serve them hot or at room temperature.

PREP TIME: 8 MINUTES
COOKING TIME: 10 MINUTES
SERVES 4

10 large eggs
¼ cup milk
4 ounces chorizo (Spanish sausage), finely chopped
3 tablespoons chopped fresh cilantro
4 ounces cream cheese, softened and cut into small pieces

In a medium bowl, whisk together the eggs and milk until just combined. You should still see large bubbles while you are whisking. Set aside.

In a large sauté pan (preferably nonstick) over medium heat, cook the sausage for 5 minutes. Add the eggs and stir constantly so they cook evenly. Just before the eggs are fully cooked, scatter the cilantro and cream cheese over the top and stir gently until desired doneness.

# Scrambled Eggs with Pepper Boursin

Who doesn't like a little cheese with their scrambled eggs? This grown-up version of the classic breakfast entrée is sure to become a new favorite. The creamy texture and intense flavor of the pepper Boursin complement the scrambled eggs perfectly.

PREP TIME: 7 MINUTES
COOKING TIME: 10 MINUTES
SERVES 2 TO 3

6 large eggs
3 tablespoons milk
1/4 teaspoon kosher salt
4 teaspoons chopped fresh chives
1 1/2 tablespoons unsalted butter
3 tablespoons Boursin cheese with pepper

In a medium bowl, whisk together the eggs, milk, salt, and chives until just combined. You should still see large bubbles while you are whisking.

In a 10-inch sauté pan (preferably nonstick), melt the butter over medium-low heat. As soon as the butter stops foaming, add the eggs. Stir the eggs with a spatula, constantly keeping them moving so they cook evenly. Just before the eggs are fully cooked, scatter the Boursin over the top, and stir gently until desired doneness.

# Sweet Basil Bacon

Sometimes you need to add a little spice to your life, especially when you seem to be stuck in a routine. A little variety can change your outlook for the whole day. Even the simplest of foods can dazzle when you change things up a bit. Try adding a little basil and brown sugar the next time you make bacon. It's as delicious at breakfast as it is on a BLT. The brown sugar caramelizes slightly, and the basil keeps it from being too sweet.

PREP TIME: 2 MINUTES
COOKING TIME: 15 MINUTES
SERVES 4

8 slices thick-cut bacon
1 tablespoon light brown sugar, packed
½ teaspoon dried basil

Preheat the oven to 375°F. Line a sheet pan with parchment paper.

Arrange the bacon slices on the sheet pan. Bake the bacon for 10 minutes and remove from the oven. Turn the bacon over and sprinkle with the brown sugar and basil. Bake for an additional 5 minutes or until crisp. Drain on paper towels and serve.

# Strawberry Butter

This is one of those "It's too easy to be a recipe" recipes. Blend your favorite preserves with butter and you have a delicious, quick topping for toast, muffins, French toast, or croissants.

PREP TIME: 5 MINUTES
MAKES 3/4 CUP

1/2 cup (1 stick) unsalted butter, at room temperature
2 tablespoons strawberry preserves

Put the butter and preserves into a food processor. Pulse on/off until well blended with a few visible pieces of fruit remaining. Serve at room temperature for the best flavor.

**NOTE:** Any fruit preserves can be substituted, but strawberry seems to be the favorite in our house. Whatever you choose, look for one with whole pieces of fruit so you end up with an interesting texture.

# Cinnamon-Maple Butter

When we first moved to Anguilla and were in the process of starting our lives over, we occasionally felt a little homesick. All it took was some of this Cinnamon-Maple Butter on our morning toast to remind us of our roots and get our minds back in focus on the future.

PREP TIME: 5 MINUTES
MAKES 3/4 CUP

1/2 cup (1 stick) unsalted butter, softened
3 tablespoons pure maple syrup
1/2 teaspoon ground cinnamon
1/4 teaspoon ground nutmeg

Combine all of the ingredients in a food processor. Pulse on/off until well blended.

# ANGUILLA MEETS VERMONT

We sometimes regret not having a larger family. Over the years, we've imagined what our house would be like—particularly at mealtime—with all of us around a large country table. Everyone would be talking at once, all of us bonded by history and love.

It took us years to realize that family is about people who care for each other. It's about relationships that develop over time and may have nothing at all to do with birth parents and ancestry. Certainly, nothing replaces the bond of a family connected by blood, but sometimes a family comes into your life unexpectedly and when it does, it is something to cherish and protect as much as life itself.

We are lucky enough to have two families. Our son Jesse and his wife Maggie bring joy into our lives more than they know. Less obvious is our Anguillan family of twelve who help make Blanchard's Restaurant what it is today. We're an unlikely group to say the least, yet so unquestionably connected that the closeness still surprises us all from time to time.

Understandably curious about winter and snow, our tropical family longed to experience what they've seen on television and heard about for years. Taking our role as surrogate parents seriously, we closed the restaurant for five days in January and all headed for the snowy hills of Vermont.

We had snowball fights and went skiing, sledding and snowmobiling; we even took the gondola to the top of Killington. But one of the most emotional images etched in our memories is having the whole family gathered around our long country table for breakfast. Our dream of a big family had come true. Now, when we look at that table, we still see Bug passing the pancakes and maple syrup, Lowell finishing up the scrambled eggs, and Ozzie and Clinton jumping up to make more bacon.

# Cranberry Coffee Cake

The only thing better than waking up to breakfast in bed may be waking up to the smell of freshly baked coffee cake. This one has an old-fashioned feel to it, highlighted by the tangy cranberries. Its moist, rich, melt-in-your-mouth flavor makes it hard to resist a second piece. It's perfect with a glass of cold milk or a cup of steaming coffee.

PREP TIME: 20 MINUTES
COOKING TIME: 50 MINUTES
SERVES 10 TO 12

FOR THE STREUSEL TOPPING

¼ cup (½ stick) unsalted butter, melted
1 cup light brown sugar, packed
2 teaspoons ground cinnamon
½ cup coarsely chopped pecans
½ cup fresh or frozen cranberries, coarsely chopped

FOR THE CAKE

2 cups all-purpose flour
1 teaspoon baking powder
1 teaspoon baking soda
½ teaspoon kosher salt
¾ cup (1½ sticks) unsalted butter, at room temperature
1 cup sugar
1 teaspoon pure vanilla extract
2 large eggs, at room temperature
1½ cups sour cream

Preheat the oven to 350°F. Butter and flour a 10-inch tube pan.

Make the topping: Combine all of the ingredients in a medium bowl. Stir until crumbly, then set aside.

Make the cake: In a small bowl, whisk together the flour, baking powder, baking soda, and salt. Set aside.

Using an electric mixer fitted with a paddle attachment, cream the butter, sugar, and vanilla until light and fluffy. Add the eggs one at a time until just incorporated. Scrape down the sides of the bowl once or twice to ensure thorough mixing.

On low speed, alternately add the flour mixture and the sour cream. Start with about one-third of the flour, then add half of the sour cream, then add another third of the flour, then the rest of the sour cream, then the remaining flour. Do not overmix.

Spread half of the cake batter in the pan. (It may not seem like enough, but don't worry.) Crumble half the topping over the top and spoon on the remaining batter. Crumble the rest of the topping over the batter and bake the cake for about 50 minutes, or until a tester inserted in the center comes out clean. Allow the cake to cool slightly on a wire rack.

Invert the cake onto a serving platter or cake stand and remove the pan.

# Starters

* Roasted Asparagus Soup
* Prosciutto Goat Cheese Roll-ups
* Mexican Corn Soup
* Brie and Artichoke Toasts
* Artichoke Dip
* Baked Goat Cheese Spread
* Mountain Salsa
* Blue Cheese and Mango Bundles
* Ricotta and Chive Spread
* Vermont Cheddar Clouds
* Chinese Chicken Skewers

# quality

When people ask us what we do for a living, we say, "We own a restaurant on the Caribbean island of Anguilla and, luckily, our staff does such an amazing job that we can spend our summers writing in Vermont." The response is almost always a sigh of longing.

A surprising number of people fantasize about starting a new life for themselves. They dream of being their own boss and running their own business. Others have no desire to change careers but sense their lives need a little fine-tuning. They're missing the passion; they want to get more of what life has to offer.

To us, whether we're preparing a meal or hiring a staff, it's all about quality. It doesn't matter if you're making a grilled cheese sandwich or searching for a new career. If you indulge yourself by seeking quality, the feeling of contentment will permeate all aspects of your life. Indulgence is often considered synonymous with being greedy and self-absorbed. We see it differently. Meaningful indulgence is about having a sense of values . . . an appreciation of the sacrifices required for a greater appreciation of life. It's about nurturing the self, but not about being selfish.

When it comes to food or lifestyle, we would rather do without than do something halfheartedly. It's so important to feed your soul with life's pleasures—both small and grand. We'll make a special trip to a local bakery so the bread on our grilled cheese sandwich has the chewy texture we love. And heaven knows, when it comes to careers, we're as fussy as they come. After starting eight businesses we've learned what matters. A perfect job is not about the money. It's about waking up in the morning and being exactly where you want to be and working with people whose company you truly enjoy. That's quality. That's living what you love.

Insisting on quality when it comes to food is easy. It's not about fancy, complicated, or exotic meals. What matters is finding the freshest available ingredients and then preparing them the best way you know how. Family and friends will notice your attention to detail and feel honored to know you care enough about them to make something delicious just for them. That love and caring brings a quality to your table and your life at the same time.

# Roasted Asparagus Soup

Presentation can be the defining characteristic between a good recipe and a spectacular dish. While we've never been ones for elaborate plate arrangements, we feel a great deal of pride when we present a beautiful dish. The pureed asparagus gives this soup a beautiful spring green color that looks spectacular in a simple white bowl.

PREP TIME: 12 MINUTES
COOKING TIME: 25 MINUTES
SERVES 4

3 pounds asparagus, trimmed and cut into 1-inch pieces
6 medium shallots, minced
3 tablespoons olive oil
Kosher salt and freshly ground black pepper
2 to 2½ cups chicken broth

FOR THE PARMESAN TOASTS
8 slices crusty baguette, sliced ½ inch thick
¼ cup freshly grated Parmesan cheese

1 tablespoon chopped fresh parsley, for garnish

Preheat the oven to 450°F. Line two sheet pans with parchment paper.

Toss the asparagus, shallots, and olive oil together on a sheet pan until thoroughly combined. Arrange in a single layer and sprinkle with salt and pepper. Roast for about 15 minutes, or until the asparagus is tender. In a small saucepan, bring the chicken broth to a simmer and set aside.

While the asparagus is roasting, arrange the bread on the other sheet pan and top each slice with a generous amount of cheese. As soon as the asparagus is removed from the oven, bake the toasts until the cheese is melted and beginning to brown.

When the asparagus is tender, transfer to a food processor and pulse to blend. With the machine running, add enough chicken broth until the soup is the consistency of light cream. Cut half of the toasts into quarters and put four quarters into each soup bowl. Pour the soup into the bowls and top each with a whole toast. Sprinkle with parsley and serve immediately.

## Prosciutto Goat Cheese Roll-ups

This is a good starter to serve to friends while they're mingling in the kitchen before dinner. It's incredibly easy to make and yet has enough flair to attract attention. We like the lively crunch of black pepper, but if you prefer a milder version, you could use your favorite herbs instead.

PREP TIME: 6 MINUTES
COOKING TIME: 6 MINUTES
SERVES 4

1 (8-ounce) goat cheese log, cut into 8 slices
2 tablespoons olive oil
2 teaspoons coarsely ground black pepper
8 slices prosciutto, sliced paper-thin, cut in half lengthwise

Preheat the oven to 425°F. Line a sheet pan with parchment paper.

Cut the goat cheese slices in half. Using a pastry brush, coat the goat cheese pieces on both sides with olive oil. Sprinkle the black pepper on one side of each piece.

Wrap each piece of cheese with a slice of prosciutto and arrange on the sheet pan. Bake for 5 to 6 minutes, or until the cheese is soft and the prosciutto begins to crisp.

# Mexican Corn Soup

This dish always reminds us of a small village we visited in Mexico. A local woman used these ingredients to create an incredible combination of flavors. It's a great way to use leftover roasted chicken, but if you don't have any, just simmer the boneless chicken breast over low heat in a small amount of salted water until it is cooked through.

PREP TIME: 15 MINUTES
COOKING TIME: 20 MINUTES
SERVES 4 AS A MAIN COURSE OR 6 AS A STARTER

2 (10-ounce) packages frozen corn, thawed and drained
1 cup chicken broth
1/4 cup (1/2 stick) unsalted butter
2 cups milk
2 medium garlic cloves, minced
2 teaspoons fresh oregano leaves or 1 teaspoon dried
3/4 teaspoon kosher salt
1/4 teaspoon freshly ground black pepper
1/4 cup diced canned green chiles
1 pound boneless chicken breasts, cooked and cut into 1/2-inch cubes
16 cherry tomatoes, quartered
8 ounces Monterey Jack cheese, cut into 1/2-inch cubes
1/4 cup chopped fresh cilantro, for garnish
1 medium bag unsalted corn tortilla chips, broken into small pieces

In a food processor, puree the corn with the chicken broth. In a large pot, melt the butter over high heat and add the corn mixture. Cover and bring to a boil, stirring often. Reduce the heat and simmer for 5 minutes, stirring several times.

Add the milk, garlic, oregano, salt, pepper, and chiles. Bring to a boil and simmer over low heat for 2 minutes. Add the chicken and tomatoes and heat through, 2 to 3 minutes.

Remove from the heat, add the cheese, and stir to blend. Ladle into bowls and top with cilantro and *generous* amounts of tortilla chips.

# Brie and Artichoke Toasts

It's easier to remove the rind from the Brie if it's very cold and firm. We usually put it in the freezer for half an hour or so to stiffen it up. For even more flavor, we often substitute St.-André cheese for the Brie.

PREP TIME: 10 MINUTES
COOKING TIME: 8 MINUTES
MAKES 20 SLICES

4 ounces Brie, very cold
1 (6-ounce) jar marinated artichoke hearts, drained and coarsely chopped (see Note)
1 baguette, cut into ½-inch slices
3 tablespoons freshly grated Parmesan cheese
2 tablespoons chopped fresh chives, for garnish

Preheat the oven to 450°F. Line a sheet pan with parchment paper.

Use a sharp knife to cut the rind from the Brie and scrape the cheese into a medium bowl. Add the chopped artichoke hearts and, using a fork, blend well.

Arrange the sliced bread in a single layer on the sheet pan and mound a tablespoon of the Brie and artichoke mixture on each. Top with Parmesan and bake for 6 minutes, or until lightly browned. Sprinkle with chives and serve immediately.

**NOTE:** Marinated artichoke hearts are readily available in supermarkets. They come packed in olive oil in small jars and are usually whole or halved. Sometimes you can find them chopped as well, which makes this recipe even easier.

# Artichoke Dip

Some of our favorite memories with friends are not formal, sit-down dinners, but casual get-togethers where everyone is eating, talking, and enjoying the moment. The chunks of artichoke in this appetizer blended with smooth sour cream will please most everyone's palate. This is a quick, delicious trick to pull out of your hat when you don't want to spend a lot of time fussing.

PREP TIME: 5 MINUTES
MAKES 1¼ CUPS

1 (8½-ounce) can artichoke hearts, drained well
¼ cup sour cream
½ teaspoon kosher salt
⅛ teaspoon freshly ground black pepper

Place all the ingredients in a food processor and puree to desired texture. We like to keep a few visible chunks but that's a matter of personal choice.

Serve chilled or at room temperature with crudités, pita chips, or premium potato chips.

# Baked Goat Cheese Spread

The Vermont Butter & Cheese Company is one of forty cheese makers in the state. For years, their award-winning goat cheese was available only in local markets. More recently, however, we've found it in stores across the country. In fact, just a few months ago we had to laugh when we bought some in our local grocery store in Anguilla.

PREP TIME: 8 MINUTES
COOKING TIME: 10 MINUTES
SERVES 6 TO 8

1 pound soft goat cheese, at room temperature
1 tablespoon fresh oregano leaves or 1 ½ teaspoons dried
1 tablespoon fresh thyme leaves or 1 ½ teaspoons dried
1 ½ teaspoons grated fresh lemon peel
About ½ cup olive oil
Coarsely ground black pepper
1 loaf crusty rustic bread, sliced ½ inch thick

Preheat the oven to 375°F.

In a large bowl, combine the goat cheese, oregano, thyme, lemon peel, and ¼ cup of the olive oil until well blended.

Transfer the cheese mixture to a shallow baking dish and top with a generous amount of coarsely ground pepper. Bake for 10 minutes.

While the cheese is baking, use 3 tablespoons of the remaining olive oil to brush one side of each bread slice. Either grill or broil until lightly browned.

Serve the cheese spread immediately with the bread.

# SALSA IN THE MOUNTAINS

How many times have you returned from a vacation wanting to re-create a recipe that you enjoyed while you were away? It happens to us all the time, and over the years we've learned that most people love to share recipes with anyone who asks.

When we traveled to Mexico with our son, Jesse, and his wife, Maggie, we spent a day on horseback in the mountains. We wanted to see the millions of monarch butterflies that migrate each winter to these few forested peaks in the middle of what feels like nowhere. It was a sanctuary, well protected from intruders and just as spectacular as you might imagine. But as miraculous as the vision of 20 million butterflies might be, we're a little embarrassed to say that it was our snack on the way back to our car that we remember most.

Our guide led us through the clouds to the dusty clearing where we'd first mounted our horses. "Hungry?" he asked. The four of us looked at each other and wondered what he could possibly have in mind. We saw no restaurant, no house, no grill, no sign of food whatsoever. Curiosity and hunger urged us to follow his lead past some rudimentary wooden stalls that looked as if they'd been abandoned long ago. He waved us behind the last stall, where he proudly introduced us to his stunning wife and five-year-old daughter, both of whom were sitting quietly on a bench in the shade.

Once we realized we were at his family's restaurant, we studied the long, weathered plank table that was the focal point of the outdoor kitchen. It was draped with a yellow flowered tablecloth and covered with a display of mismatched bowls, each filled with a single ingredient: tomatillos, cilantro, chiles, onions, cornmeal, and avocados. There was a large stone mortar and pestle and an old gas stove with a pot of tomatillos simmering in a little water.

It was as though this little family had allowed us to be part of their dream. They had set up

shop to feed people in the mountains and welcomed us to share the experience. The woman greeted us shyly and began what was probably a routine demonstration. With nobody else in sight, however, we felt as though we were the first visitors to stumble upon this enchanting scene. Her slender hands kneaded a coarse mixture of cornmeal and water that was in a bright turquoise enamel pot. When the mixture held together, she pulled off a piece, rolled it into a ball, and placed it on a well-worn wooden tortilla press. She pulled the lever down and in seconds placed a perfectly formed tortilla onto a nearby plate.

As she started to repeat the process, we motioned to the press and she nodded with approval, allowing us to join in. She spoke no English and we spoke little Spanish, but it didn't matter. By the time we were through, we were making tortillas, cooking them on a griddle, slicing avocados, and grinding the tomatillos into fresh green salsa. The little girl was wearing a white cotton dress embroidered with pink flowers and green trim. It blew gracefully in the breeze as she played hide-and-seek around the outside of the building.

Eating has as much to do with environment as with the flavor of the food. Travel provides countless opportunities to discover new flavors from people who cook what they love and enjoy sharing that moment with new friends. Nothing can precisely replace the taste of those warm corn tortillas filled with avocado and green salsa at an altitude of ten thousand feet.

Every time we make this salsa at home, we see that little girl with her jet-black hair and bright white dress dancing around as if on air.

# Mountain Salsa

Some recipes require special preparation. The difference between making this in a blender or food processor as opposed to using a mortar and pestle is like night and day. Even if you are careful, the tomatillos will become watery in a blender and the sauce loses its wonderful texture. Large mortar and pestles made from volcanic rock are readily available in specialty kitchen stores these days. Once you've used one, you'll wonder how you lived without it.

PREP TIME: 5 MINUTES
COOKING TIME: 10 MINUTES
MAKES 1 CUP

12 tomatillos, husks removed
2 serrano chiles, finely chopped
1 small garlic clove
1 tablespoon finely chopped onion
1/4 cup fresh cilantro leaves
Kosher salt and freshly ground black pepper

Place the tomatillos in a medium saucepan and cover with water. Cover the pot and bring to a boil. Reduce the heat to low and simmer for 10 minutes, or until soft and tender.

Using a large mortar and pestle, grind together the chiles, garlic, onion, and cilantro. Add the drained tomatillos and continue to grind until well blended. Add salt and pepper to taste and mix well.

**NOTE:** This is a great sauce with many, many uses. Serve it as a dip with tortilla chips, spoon some into your favorite omelet, or use as a topping for tacos, enchiladas, or burritos. And, of course, you can duplicate our day in the mountains of Mexico and warm a few corn tortillas in a dry pan and roll them around some sliced avocado and a generous spoonful of the salsa.

Blanchard's

# Blue Cheese and Mango Bundles

Sweet and spicy chutney, salty prosciutto, and robust blue cheese create a deliciously unique combination of flavors. If your prosciutto is very moist, these bundles will hold together just fine. Some can be on the drier side; if that's the case, just use a toothpick to secure the rolls.

PREP TIME: 15 MINUTES
MAKES 16 BUNDLES

8 thin slices prosciutto
1 cup arugula leaves
⅓ cup good-quality mango chutney
2 ounces blue cheese, crumbled

Arrange the prosciutto in a single layer on a cutting board and cut each slice in half crosswise.

Place 1 or 2 arugula leaves on each piece of prosciutto, allowing the round end of the leaf to stick out past the prosciutto on one side. Top each with ½ teaspoon of the chutney and sprinkle the cheese over the top, pressing lightly to keep it from falling out.

Roll each piece tightly into a cylinder and serve at room temperature.

**NOTE:** These bundles can be made up to 6 hours in advance and kept covered in the refrigerator. Bring to room temperature before serving.

# Ricotta and Chive Spread

When we have guests for dinner, they tend to expect an elaborate meal that takes hours to prepare. Much to their surprise, they're delighted with the easy dishes we serve. While we spend many hours or even days perfecting a recipe, the result is usually a simple dish that anyone can prepare. This quick dip is delicious served on slices of grilled bread and topped with a few extra chives for garnish. If you're looking for something even quicker, use some sesame or poppy-seed crackers.

PREP TIME: 5 MINUTES
MAKES 1 ½ CUPS

1 ½ cups ricotta cheese
8 drops Tabasco sauce
½ teaspoon Worcestershire sauce
¾ teaspoon kosher salt
¼ teaspoon freshly ground black pepper
5 tablespoons chopped fresh chives
2 to 3 teaspoons olive oil

In a small bowl, combine the cheese, Tabasco, Worcestershire, salt, pepper, and chives. Transfer the mixture to a serving bowl, drizzle with the oil, and serve.

# Vermont Cheddar Clouds

We've traveled across the world, discovered many different tastes, and love sharing cultural traditions. Sometimes, however, the best food is right at home. Pile these in a napkin-lined basket as guests arrive and they'll be gone in a minute. If you make them ahead of time, keep them covered in the refrigerator for up to two days and reheat on a sheet pan before serving.

PREP TIME: 12 MINUTES
COOKING TIME: 30 MINUTES
MAKES 18

¼ cup (½ stick) unsalted butter
½ cup all-purpose flour
2 large eggs
¼ teaspoon kosher salt
4 drops Tabasco sauce
4 ounces Vermont sharp Cheddar cheese, shredded
½ teaspoon poppy seeds

Preheat the oven to 375°F. Line two sheet pans with parchment paper.

Place the butter and 1 cup water into a large saucepan over high heat and bring to a boil. Reduce the heat to medium, add the flour, and whisk constantly for 3 minutes, or until the dough holds together and pulls away from the sides of the pan. Remove from the heat.

Add the eggs one at a time, whisking well after each addition. The batter should form soft peaks when lifted up with a spoon. Add the salt, Tabasco, cheese, and poppy seeds and mix gently to blend.

Spoon tablespoons of the batter 2 inches apart onto the sheet pan. Bake for 30 minutes or until golden brown. Serve warm.

**NOTE:** Vermont Cheddar can range from mild to extra sharp and is aged from one to five years. We attended a cheese-tasting at the Grafton Village Cheese Company and were surprised to learn that the flavor of each varies dramatically. Our personal favorite was a sharp cheese aged for three years.

# Chinese Chicken Skewers

We like to serve these aromatic skewers on a bed of greens tossed with the Classic Mustard Vinaigrette on page 59. If you're passing them at a party, try drizzling a small amount of the vinaigrette on top instead. They're delicious cold too, so don't worry if you have a few leftovers.

PREP TIME: 20 MINUTES
COOKING TIME: 8 MINUTES
SERVES 6

1 dozen 6-inch bamboo skewers
½ cup olive oil
1 teaspoon minced garlic
2 teaspoons Chinese five-spice powder
2 teaspoons ground cumin
2 teaspoons ground coriander
2 teaspoons toasted sesame seeds
1 teaspoon kosher salt
1½ cups dried unflavored bread crumbs (see page 10)
1 pound boneless chicken breasts, cut into strips 1 × 3 × ½ inch thick

Soak the skewers in water for at least 30 minutes to keep them from burning.

Prepare the grill or preheat the broiler. If broiling, line a sheet pan with parchment paper.

In a small bowl, combine the olive oil, garlic, five-spice powder, cumin, coriander, sesame seeds, salt, and bread crumbs. Weave the chicken strips onto the skewers, piercing each strip in three places to keep it secure.

Coat the chicken thoroughly with the bread-crumb mixture, pressing firmly. Grill or broil for 3 to 4 minutes on each side, or until cooked through and golden brown.

# Salads

* Caesar Coleslaw
* Leek Salad
* Zucchini Salad
* Roasted Carrot Salad
* Classic Mustard Vinaigrette
* Basil-Roasted Plum Tomatoes
* Creamy Sesame Dressing
* Pistachio-Crusted Goat Cheese Salad
* Chilled Asparagus Salad

# $4,000 and a blender

Before we had Blanchard's Restaurant we made salad dressing for a living. We actually had no idea what we were getting into, but in 1983 the specialty food industry was coming to life and we jumped right in. We'd had a rough year and found ourselves unemployed, strapped with a double mortgage, car payment, and $4,000 that probably should have gone to the bank. In fact, we were terrified that the bank would come to collect what they believed to be theirs. In a last-ditch effort to protect ourselves, we buried our $4,000 in a little metal box under Jesse's swing set. (Not an easy task in Vermont when the temperatures are subzero and the ground is frozen solid.)

We needed a new beginning. The first step before allowing ourselves to unearth the money was to make a list of our personal aspirations and goals. We examined our life and thought hard about what we should do. Determined to stay in Vermont, we wanted to work together and create a life that allowed us to spend as much time as possible with Jesse. He was in third grade and we wanted to be part of his life more than traditional jobs would allow. We dreamed about taking wonderful trips together during school vacations and cringed at the thought of having to ask a supervisor for permission to attend school plays, soccer games, and ski races. As if that weren't enough of a challenge, we were determined to create a lifestyle filled with passion. We believed then—and now—that if you love what you do, it's not a job.

Luckily, it didn't take long to determine that our passion for food might be the answer to earning a living. The wolves were at the door and we had no time for extensive analysis and business plans. We did our own style of market research, took a deep breath, and followed our instincts.

After several weeks of studying the competition and testing hundreds of recipes, we concluded that, as always, quality would set us apart from the rest. We bought the finest olive oil, aged vinegars, and ingredients with no added preservatives. Our Lemon-Pepper Vinaigrette was loaded with fresh lemon juice, and we carefully toasted the seeds for our Sesame Seed Dressing in small batches to make sure it was done to our liking. If our dream was to create a line of specialty foods, we were going to do it the best way we knew how.

In a matter of months, we were making salad dressings in a blender and selling them to Bloomingdale's, Macy's, and about 2,500 specialty food stores across the country. (Don't you love happy endings?)

# Caesar Coleslaw

Summer barbecues are a wonderful way to bring friends, family, and neighbors together to celebrate the arrival of warmer weather. Coleslaw is a great side dish to serve with burgers, steaks, or barbecued chicken, and a delicious topping for sandwiches all year long. As much as we love the traditional version, this twist on the classic has become our recipe of choice when we fire up the grill.

**PREP TIME: 30 MINUTES**
**SERVES 6 TO 8**

FOR THE DRESSING

1 cup Hellmann's mayonnaise
¾ teaspoon anchovy paste
1 teaspoon Worcestershire sauce
3½ tablespoons fresh lemon juice
2 medium garlic cloves, minced
¾ teaspoon coarsely cracked black pepper

FOR THE SLAW

1½ pounds Chinese napa cabbage, cored and thinly sliced (8 cups)
½ pound red cabbage, cored and thinly sliced (2 cups)
½ pound jicama, peeled and cut into long, thin strips (see Note)
2 large carrots, shredded or grated
4 scallions, thinly sliced (green and white parts)

½ cup freshly shredded Parmesan cheese

In a small mixing bowl, whisk all of the dressing ingredients until well blended.

In a large bowl, toss together both cabbages, jicama, carrots, and scallions. Add enough dressing to coat well. Add the Parmesan and toss again.

**NOTE:** Jicama (pronounced hicama) is an underused, mild-flavored vegetable that adds a refreshing crunch to any salad.

# Leek Salad

Leeks are used far more often in other countries than in the United States. Typically, we've sautéed them and served them warm with seafood. Though less conventional, we love this alternative preparation. Simmering the leeks in wine enhances their naturally subtle flavor, and the lime juice adds a spark not usually associated with this mild vegetable.

PREP TIME: 10 MINUTES
COOKING TIME: 20 MINUTES
SERVES 4

6 leeks
3 tablespoons olive oil
½ cup chicken or vegetable broth
½ cup dry white wine
1 tablespoon fresh lime juice
1 teaspoon Dijon mustard
2 tablespoons chopped fresh dill
2 tablespoons chopped fresh chives
Kosher salt and freshly ground black pepper

Trim off the dark green leaves of the leeks and discard. Cut the white and pale green part in half lengthwise, rinse well, and dry.

In a large sauté pan, heat 2 tablespoons of the oil over medium-high heat until hot but not smoking. Add the leeks and cook until lightly browned, 5 to 6 minutes, turning occasionally. Add the broth and wine. Cover, reduce the heat to medium, and cook for 10 minutes or until tender. Transfer to a platter.

In a small bowl, whisk together the remaining tablespoon of oil, the lime juice, mustard, dill, and chives. Stir the herb mixture into the pan juices and continue stirring over medium heat for 1 minute. Return the leeks to the pan and coat well with the herb mixture. Season with salt and pepper to taste. Serve at room temperature or chilled.

# Zucchini Salad

We're always searching for new ways to prepare zucchini, and orange peel gives this salad a refreshing twist. We also use the dressing as a sauce for grilled fish. Just spoon a little on right before serving and let it melt into the fish for a minute or two.

**PREP TIME: 10 MINUTES**
**SERVES 6**

¼ cup sour cream
¼ cup Hellmann's mayonnaise
1 teaspoon grated fresh orange peel
1 teaspoon dried basil
½ teaspoon kosher salt
¼ teaspoon freshly ground black pepper
2 pounds small zucchini, ends trimmed

In a small bowl, whisk together the sour cream, mayonnaise, orange peel, basil, salt, and pepper. Set aside.

Slice the zucchini into very thin rounds, either by hand or in a food processor. Place the sliced zucchini in a large bowl and toss with enough dressing to coat. Serve chilled or at room temperature.

# Roasted Carrot Salad

Roasting carrots intensifies their natural sweetness far more than boiling does because the flavor and nutrients are not lost in the water, and it's just as easy. Tossing the carrots with the seasonings while they're still warm gives you an additional burst of flavor as well.

PREP TIME: 10 MINUTES
COOKING TIME: 20 MINUTES
SERVES 6

2 pounds carrots, peeled
3 tablespoons olive oil
Kosher salt and freshly ground black pepper
2 tablespoons balsamic vinegar
¼ teaspoon ground cumin

Preheat the oven to 400°F. Line a sheet pan with parchment paper.

Cut the carrots into 2-inch lengths. If they are very large, cut the thicker ends in half lengthwise. Place the carrots on the sheet pan and toss with the olive oil and a generous amount of salt and pepper. Arrange the carrots in a single layer on the pan and roast until tender, 15 to 20 minutes.

Transfer the carrots to a bowl and toss immediately with the vinegar and cumin. Allow to cool and serve at room temperature.

# Classic Mustard Vinaigrette

Have you ever had a salad tossed with a vinaigrette that seems to have no flavor? When friends ask us for a good, basic salad dressing recipe, this is the one we recommend. This dressing never gets lost on a salad and always gets rave reviews.

**PREP TIME: 5 MINUTES**
**MAKES 1 CUP**

3 tablespoons balsamic vinegar
3 tablespoons Dijon mustard
½ cup olive oil
½ cup vegetable oil
¼ teaspoon kosher salt
⅛ teaspoon freshly ground black pepper

In a medium bowl, whisk the vinegar and mustard until blended.

Slowly add both oils, whisking continually until just emulsified. If you mix it too long, the dressing will become too thick to pour. Add the salt and pepper.

# YOU DON'T HAVE TO MOW A GARDEN

Many of our friends in Vermont have gardens. Some just have a few herbs outside the kitchen door; others have ambitious plots of land tilled and planted with enough produce to feed the whole town. Most are located on a level piece of ground in the middle of a lawn or field.

We don't have much flat land on our property. Our house is built on a quiet dirt road that happens to be on a mountain where level ground is at a premium. When we first bought the land, we recognized that if we wanted a lawn, we'd have to forgo the idea of a garden.

Once we built the house, we started to think more about landscaping. We seeded the lawn, planted some crabapple trees, and cleared some of the woods to open up more of the view. We built a stone retaining wall and intended to plant more lawn on the sloped land above it, but dreaded the thought of mowing it. It was an awkward area and we found ourselves procrastinating when it came to seeding the lawn.

Saturdays in our town always call for a trip to the farmer's market. We'd load up with bags of perfect tomatoes and piles of fresh herbs. Though we love the market, we grew increasingly discouraged about not having our own garden. Loving food as much as we do, it just didn't seem right. Nothing can replace plucking a ripe tomato from the vine or cutting the dill right before it gets tossed into a salad.

Then one day an idea hit us head-on. Wouldn't it be beautiful to plant vegetables along the top of the stone wall? Where is it written that a garden has to be flat? And why exactly do you need long rows of vegetables? We had a seventy-five-foot-long by six-foot-wide strip of sloped land above the stone wall that would certainly look more spectacular cov-

ered with vegetables than with grass. The more we thought about it, the more we felt vegetables would look even better than the expensive plants traditionally used for this kind of landscaping.

We planted a palette of greens with as many textures as we could find. Lettuce comes in so many varieties that it's hard to imagine anything prettier when they're all mixed together. We interspersed the lettuce with dark spinach leaves, broadleaf bok choy, and feathery fronds of dill, and backed it up with a taller row of peas and tomato plants to make it more interesting.

The fun part is that it takes a while for visitors to notice that we even have a vegetable garden. Once they do, they feel as if they've discovered a secret because it's so much a part of the landscape. We love inviting our friends without gardens to come pick for themselves. (There's always more than we can eat.) And every time we mow the lawn we smile up at the garden, grateful for not having to mow that awkward slope.

# Basil-Roasted Plum Tomatoes

Roasted tomatoes can be served as a wonderful side salad, but we often keep some in the refrigerator to use in a variety of other ways. Coarsely chopped, they make a great addition to pasta, omelets, and soups.

**PREP TIME: 2 MINUTES**
**COOKING TIME: 20 MINUTES**
**SERVES 8**

8 ripe plum tomatoes, cut in half lengthwise
Kosher salt and freshly ground black pepper
16 whole fresh basil leaves
¼ cup olive oil

Preheat the oven to 400°F. Line a sheet pan with parchment paper.

Arrange the tomato halves cut side up on the sheet pan. Sprinkle with salt and pepper and scatter the basil leaves on top. Drizzle with olive oil.

Roast until soft and lightly browned, about 20 minutes. Serve at room temperature.

# Creamy Sesame Dressing

This is an all-purpose dressing with a little heft. Unlike a light vinaigrette, which often seems to disappear on pasta or potato salad, this more substantial dressing holds its own with those heartier combinations, as well as when tossed in a bowl of leafy greens. The robust flavor is due in part to the tahini, which gives the dressing an extra boost of sesame flavor.

**PREP TIME: 5 MINUTES**
**MAKES 1 ¼ CUPS**

1 small garlic clove
¼ cup fresh lemon juice
¼ cup soy sauce
½ cup tahini (sesame paste), stirred well
1 teaspoon roasted sesame oil
2 tablespoons sugar
½ teaspoon freshly ground black pepper

With the motor running, drop the garlic into the feed tube of a food processor and mince well. Remove the cover and add ¼ cup water and all of the remaining ingredients. Puree until smooth.

# Pistachio-Crusted Goat Cheese Salad

This is one of our most popular salads. The pistachio crust on the goat cheese turns golden brown when cooked and offers a delicious contrast to the simple greens.

**PREP TIME: 8 MINUTES**
**COOKING TIME: 5 MINUTES**
**SERVES 4**

FOR THE DRESSING

⅓ cup balsamic vinegar
1 small garlic clove, minced
½ teaspoon kosher salt
½ teaspoon freshly ground black pepper
⅔ cup olive oil

4 large handfuls of mixed baby salad greens

FOR THE GOAT CHEESE

¼ cup coarsely chopped pistachio nuts
2 tablespoons dried bread crumbs (see page 10.)
2 (4-ounce) goat cheese logs, cut into ½-inch slices
1 tablespoon olive oil

8 whole chives

In a small bowl, whisk together the vinegar, garlic, salt, and pepper. Gradually whisk in the oil until well blended. In a large bowl, toss greens with just enough dressing to coat. Divide among four plates and set aside.

Mix the pistachio nuts and bread crumbs in a shallow bowl. Dredge the sliced cheese on both sides with the nut mixture, pressing gently so it adheres.

In a medium sauté pan, heat the olive oil over medium heat until hot but not smoking. Gently place the goat cheese rounds into the pan and cook for 2 minutes on each side.

Place the cheese on top of each plate of greens. Garnish each with 2 whole chives and serve immediately.

# Chilled Asparagus Salad

We've tried a great many salad dressings over the years. This sauce made with yogurt, mustard, and dill is a fabulous summer dressing. It works well with almost any vegetable—we often toss it in a bowl with freshly steamed peas or drizzle it over a platter of grilled onions and peppers.

**PREP TIME: 10 MINUTES**
**COOKING TIME: 6 MINUTES**
**SERVES 4**

2 pounds asparagus, trimmed
1 cup plain yogurt
2 tablespoons Dijon mustard
3 tablespoons chopped fresh dill
5 drops Tabasco sauce
½ teaspoon kosher salt
⅛ teaspoon freshly ground black pepper

Fill a large bowl with ice water and set aside. In a deep sauté pan, bring 1 inch of lightly salted water to a boil. Add the asparagus and cook until crisp-tender, 2 to 6 minutes depending on size. Drain and plunge immediately into the ice water to stop cooking.

In a small bowl, whisk together the yogurt, mustard, dill, Tabasco, salt, and pepper. Refrigerate until ready to serve.

Dry the asparagus and refrigerate until cold. When ready to serve, arrange the asparagus on a platter and spoon the sauce over the top.

BLANCHARD

# Sandwiches

* Chicken Feta Baguettes
* Portobellos with Peppers and Brie
* Egg Salad on Rye
* Black Forest Ham with Gruyère, Avocado, and Slaw
* Turkey with Cheddar and Lemon-Cilantro Mayonnaise
* Grilled Gruyère and Olives

# food in new york

Anguilla attracts a discerning clientele. They are discriminating travelers with a clear image of what constitutes a great dining experience. They appreciate well-prepared food and for the most part believe that attentive service and a great wine list are synonymous with fine dining. Luckily, Blanchard's meets those expectations and they come back year after year.

Many of our customers are from New York City and are curious about where we like to eat when we travel to their hometown. They are often surprised when we list our favorite haunts. We typically avoid

the five-star, five-course extravaganzas found in the city's most notable dining arenas. To us, food in New York is exciting

because people have come from all over the world to share flavors from across the globe. We love New York and we love to eat. Luckily, the two go together perfectly.

When time is tight, we narrow down our choices during the drive from Vermont. The Indian flavors at Tabla are heavenly, but then again the guacamole at Rosa Mexicana is pretty outrageous. We love the lemon chicken at Shun Lee, but it's been a while since we've had Greek food, so maybe we should try Milos. For lunch, more times than not we end up at Union Square Café, as much for its genuinely friendly staff as for Michael Romano's skill in the kitchen. Or we go to Sunrise Seafood in Chinatown for dim sum. Mind you, most tables here are round banquet style as they are in China, and the ambience is one of authenticity, not elegance. But the bok choy stir-fried with ginger at the table, and the dumplings filled with roast pork, or shrimp with crispy water chestnuts are fabulous.

As far as food that's indigenous to New York—that's easy. We'll often grab a hot dog with mustard and sauerkraut while window-shopping on Madison Avenue or have a slice of pizza after a meeting with our publisher. And there's nothing like a turkey on rye with coleslaw and Russian dressing at one of those landmark Seventh Avenue delis. And once we discovered the decadent cookies at Levain Bakery, we were hooked for good.

# Chicken Feta Baguettes

There's no need to spend time cooking chicken for sandwiches. If you have leftover roasted chicken, this is the perfect way to use it. Otherwise, just buy one or two rotisserie chickens from your local market and take it from there. The feta adds a distinctively Greek flair to the traditional chicken sandwich.

PREP TIME: 10 MINUTES
SERVES 4

8 ounces crumbled feta cheese
2 scallions, sliced thinly (green and white parts)
16 cherry tomatoes, quartered
2 small baguettes, each cut in half
2 tablespoons balsamic vinegar
¼ cup olive oil
1 pound cooked chicken (meat from 1 small chicken), sliced

In a small bowl, combine the feta and scallions until mixed well. Add the tomatoes and toss gently to distribute evenly.

Slice the baguettes horizontally and drizzle the vinegar and oil over the cut sides of each piece of bread. Arrange the sliced chicken on the bottom half of each baguette. Sprinkle with the feta mixture and cover with the top piece of bread. Cut and serve.

# Portobellos with Peppers and Brie

Roasted portobellos have a substantial, meaty taste and are full of flavor. Combine them with the creamy Brie and the texture is amazing. We really like the comforting consistency of the ingredients in this sandwich; there's nothing crunchy or distracting to take away from delicious simplicity.

PREP TIME: 8 MINUTES
COOKING TIME: 10 MINUTES
SERVES 4

8 ounces Brie (see Note)
1 ½ teaspoons Dijon mustard
4 portobello mushroom caps
Olive oil
8 (½-inch) slices sourdough or other rustic country bread
8 ounces roasted red peppers from a jar

Preheat the oven to 400°F. Line a sheet pan with parchment paper.

Use a sharp knife to slice the rind from the Brie and place the cheese into a medium bowl. Using a fork, blend the mustard into the Brie.

Arrange the mushrooms on the sheet pan and brush lightly with olive oil. Roast for 10 minutes, or until tender when pierced with a fork. Cut the mushrooms into ¼-inch-thick slices.

Spread the Brie onto 4 slices of bread. Arrange the portobello slices over the cheese and top with the red peppers. Cover the sandwiches with the remaining bread. Cut in half diagonally and serve.

NOTE: It's easier to remove the rind from the Brie if it's very cold. Half an hour in the freezer does wonders.

# Egg Salad on Rye

To us, old-fashioned egg salad tastes best on good-quality rye bread with caraway seeds. We add a little mustard for flavor, but that's all. No celery, onions, olives, or any of the other frequently used ingredients. If we're feeling indulgent, however, the optional bacon is definitely worth the effort.

PREP TIME: 8 MINUTES
COOKING TIME: 15 MINUTES
SERVES 4

8 large eggs
¼ cup Hellmann's mayonnaise
4 teaspoons Dijon mustard
Kosher salt and freshly ground black pepper
8 slices thick-cut bacon, crisply cooked and crumbled (optional)
8 slices rye bread with caraway seeds

Place the eggs in a single layer in a saucepan and cover with 1 inch of cold water. Bring to a boil over high heat. As soon as the water boils, remove the pan from the heat and let sit, covered, for exactly 15 minutes. Meanwhile, prepare a bowl of ice water and set aside. When the eggs are ready, plunge them into the ice water to stop them from overcooking.

Peel the eggs. Rinse and dry them well and place them in a medium bowl. Using a potato masher or a fork, mash the eggs to the desired consistency. Add the mayonnaise, mustard, and salt and pepper to taste and blend well. Add the crumbled bacon if desired.

Divide the salad among 4 slices of bread. Cover the sandwiches with the remaining bread, cut in half diagonally, and serve.

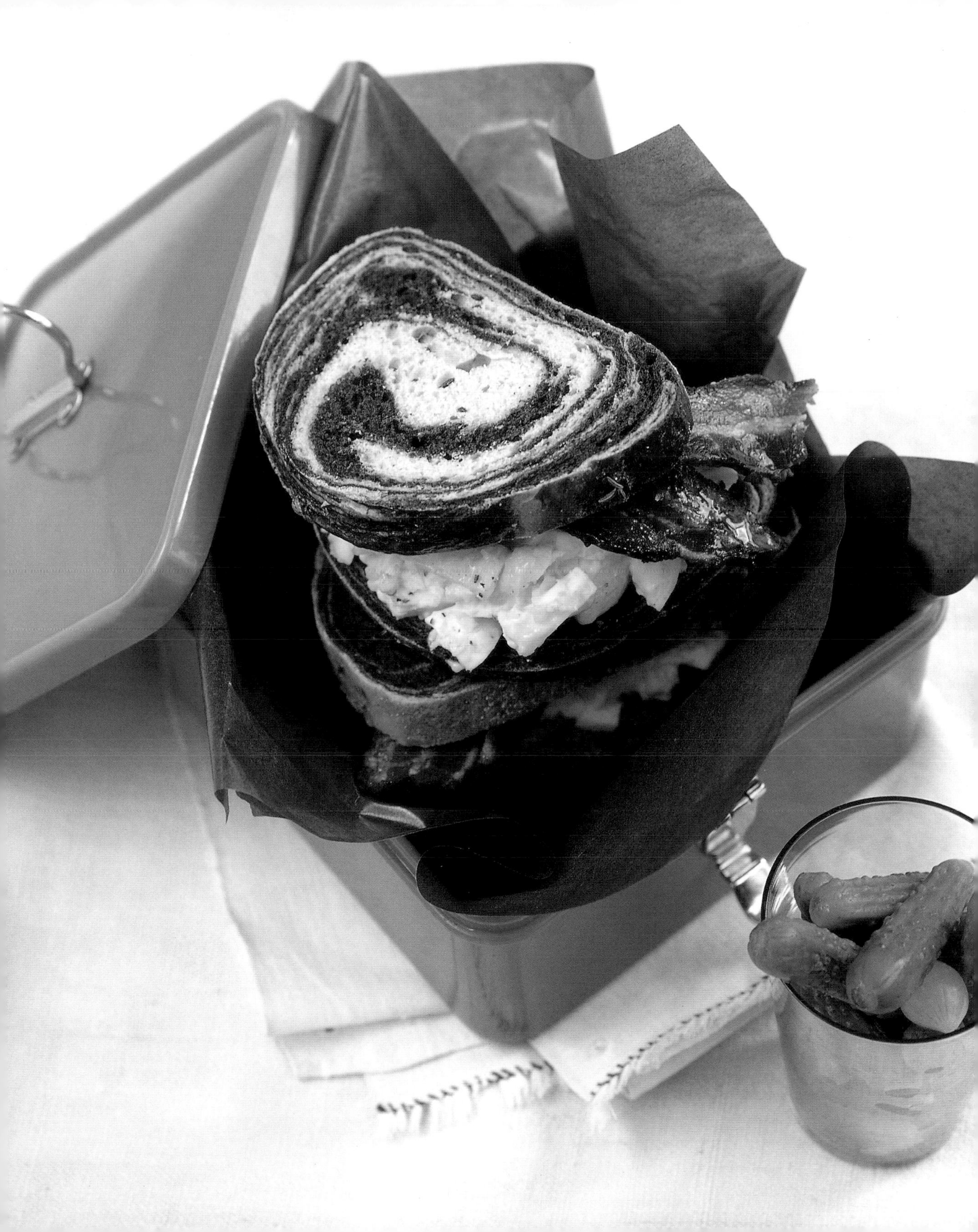

## DREAMING IN MAINE

Everyone knows there are just not enough hours in each day. We wake up in the morning with great intentions. In our case it might go something like this: "If we work on the book proposal until 2 P.M. we'll still be able to answer e-mails, mow the lawn, create a floor diagram for Christmas dinner reservations, order more fresh berries for a wedding next week, prepare for a 5 P.M. conference call, and work on the Thanksgiving menu." In reality, our agendas often get put off until the following day—or week—or even longer.

The crazy part about our overloaded life is that we absolutely love it. There's nothing we do that isn't by choice. We've worked hard to get here and have no regrets at all about how we spend our time. Unfortunately, we still can't squeeze enough into each day.

The key to a happy life is knowing how to prioritize. What's important and what can wait? That's the tricky part. It's all important and nothing should wait. What we've learned is that no matter how long our "to do" list is, there's one essential item that should always be included: "Think about how to get more out of life." Not a typical task to put on a list, perhaps, but that's why so many people don't ever get around to doing it.

We've come up with a plan that seems to work. We run away from home. Not for long, of course—just enough to give us perspective and get something done at the same time. For us, that means driving over to the coast of Maine for lunch.

Sound frivolous? It's a two-hour trip and we accomplish more in that time than we ever would during the same two hours at home. We take back roads so the drive is leisurely and relaxed. It sort of tricks our brains into thinking we're on vacation. It's amazing how peaceful, uninterrupted time gets our creative juices going. We take turns driving while the other one makes notes about whatever we're discussing.

Often, we end up talking about our life. We think about what's working and what's not. Pulling away from our usual routine for a day allows us to clarify and evaluate how we spend our time. Intuitively, we make lists of pros and cons wondering what it would be like if we made a change. Our changes aren't always as big as you might think. Sure, sometimes we come up with something huge, like moving to the Caribbean. But usually, it's more about whether or not we should hire an extra person

in the kitchen to make things go more smoothly or whether it would be smart to take out a second mortgage so we don't have to worry so much about the bills.

Dreaming about how to improve the quality of our life is how we ended up spending summers in Vermont and winters in Anguilla. We gave ourselves the luxury of time to think about what we really wanted to do. When was the last time you took a break to envision how your life might be better—to allow yourself to dream?

For us, part of what makes our dream time work is that we often go to the same place. We don't waste time thinking about where to go or what to do. We head straight for Barnacle Billy's in Ogunquit and sit on the deck overlooking the harbor. The slate tables are warmed by the sun and our shoulders drop another notch. Our cell phone is turned off while we talk about the details of our life and how to make each little element as good as it can be.

It's no coincidence that many of our major life decisions have been made over chowder, steamed clams, and lobster rolls. The combination of great food and getting away—even for just one day—creates a fresh flow of ideas that can't be duplicated at work or at home.

Figure out where you could go for a day of dreaming. Think about a great lunch in a casual setting and make sure it's a place where you can linger. Food truly does help the process. Eating what you love makes you smile and adds to the experience. Take some time getting there, too. Whether it's a long walk to a picnic in the park or a drive in the country to your favorite barbecue joint, the journey is as important as the destination. Let your mind wander about what really makes you happy. Allow yourself to think about change. If some part of your life was modified, how would it affect you?

Indulge yourself with a day of dreaming, and you're off and running. That's the first step to a life filled with passion and enthusiasm—not to mention some memorable meals along the way.

# Black Forest Ham with Gruyère, Avocado, and Slaw

Avocados have a wonderful flavor that we love in sandwiches. When we have time, we use the Caesar Coleslaw on page 54 for this sandwich. If you're in a hurry, just buy some coleslaw at your local deli—you'll still love the results.

PREP TIME: 10 MINUTES
SERVES 4

1 pound Black Forest ham, thinly sliced
8 (½-inch) slices sourdough or other rustic country bread
6 ounces Gruyère cheese, thinly sliced
2 ripe avocados, peeled, pitted, and sliced
1 cup coleslaw

Separate the slices of ham and fold them loosely onto 4 slices of the bread. Arrange the cheese over the ham and top with the avocados and slaw. Cover the sandwiches with the remaining bread, cut in half diagonally, and serve.

# Turkey with Cheddar and Lemon-Cilantro Mayonnaise

Mel has experimented in the kitchen since she was a young girl, so you know she never took a plain turkey sandwich to school for lunch. Even as a child, she loved this bold, lemony mayonnaise. Never being one to shy away from flavor, she uses a sharp Cheddar here, too. It has more *oomph* than the milder varieties.

PREP TIME: 10 MINUTES
SERVES 4

3⁄4 cup Hellmann's mayonnaise
1 teaspoon grated fresh lemon peel
1 tablespoon fresh lemon juice
1 tablespoon minced peeled fresh ginger
1⁄2 teaspoon Worcestershire sauce
2 tablespoons minced fresh cilantro
8 (1⁄2-inch) slices sourdough or other rustic country bread
1 pound thinly sliced turkey breast
4 ounces Cheddar cheese, thinly sliced

In a small bowl, whisk together the mayonnaise, lemon peel, lemon juice, ginger, Worcestershire, and cilantro.

Spread 1 tablespoon of the mayonnaise onto each slice of bread to cover the surface. Arrange the turkey slices loosely over the mayonnaise. Top with the cheese. Cover the sandwiches with the remaining bread, cut in half diagonally, and serve.

# Grilled Gruyère and Olives

Tapenade is a delicious combination of chopped olives, capers, lemon juice, olive oil, garlic, and anchovies. While you can easily make your own, we usually use a prepared version to save time. If you're not an anchovy lover, please don't let that stop you from trying this recipe. They blend in perfectly here and you won't be disappointed.

PREP TIME: 6 MINUTES
COOKING TIME: 8 MINUTES
SERVES 4

8 ounces Gruyère cheese, sliced very thin
8 (½-inch) slices sourdough or other rustic country bread
2 tablespoons tapenade
1 tablespoon unsalted butter, or more as needed

Arrange the Gruyère on 4 of the bread slices and spread each one with ½ tablespoon of the tapenade. Cover with the remaining slices of bread.

In a large, heavy skillet or griddle, melt the butter over medium heat. When the butter stops foaming, carefully transfer the sandwiches to the pan. When the bottom side is golden brown (about 4 minutes), gently turn the sandwiches and add more butter to the pan if necessary. Continue to cook until the cheese is melted and the second side is golden brown, 3 to 4 minutes or longer.

Cut in half diagonally and serve.

# Pasta

* Penne with Ricotta and Spinach
* Linguine with Scallops
* Simple, Perfect Spaghetti
* Linguine with Clams

# the magic of a table

**Why is the dining table** the most important piece of furniture in your home? Whether yours is in a formal room of its own or tucked in a corner of the kitchen, it has the extraordinary power to strengthen your family and build friendships. The tradition of sharing a meal together allows us to nurture and love each other through food.

If your family is always on the run and everyone eats according to his or her own schedule, think about sitting down and eating together more often. Better yet, get everyone involved in the kitchen, too. It's not about what you cook, it's *why* you cook.

It's about preserving a rapidly vanishing tradition that's as important to the family as the family unit itself.

Meals don't have to be complicated or fancy. Simple, straightforward recipes can fit into even the busiest lifestyles. More than just a place to eat, the family table creates a community of friends and flavors. Every night, we are lucky enough to bring people together around a table at our restaurant, and we savor the opportunity to cook for them, to visit with them, and to learn from them. The table hosts laughter and conversations—the reflections of the day—while presenting the gift of food we make for each other.

Instead of worrying about what to serve company or how quickly you can throw dinner together at the end of the day, make each meal a joyful celebration no matter how simple it may be. It's gathering people together that makes the occasion special.

# Penne with Ricotta and Spinach

Adding fresh spinach to penne is a wonderful trick that can bring vibrant color to an otherwise dull pasta. The olive oil and ricotta in this recipe replace a more traditional sauce, giving you a creamy, comforting dish that is easy to put together yet has an outstanding taste.

PREP TIME: 15 MINUTES
COOKING TIME: 15 MINUTES
SERVES 4

1 pound penne pasta
3 tablespoons olive oil
½ teaspoon kosher salt
¼ teaspoon freshly ground black pepper
6 ounces baby spinach leaves
1 cup ricotta cheese
¼ cup fresh basil leaves, cut into strips (see Note)
¼ cup chopped fresh parsley
1½ cups freshly grated Parmesan cheese

Bring a large pot of lightly salted water to a boil over high heat. Add the penne and cook until tender but still firm. (Tasting is the only way to know for sure.) Drain well and return to the pot.

With the heat on very low, add the olive oil, salt, pepper, spinach, ricotta, basil, parsley, and 1 cup of the Parmesan to the penne and mix well. Heat gently, stirring occasionally. As soon as the spinach is wilted, about 2 minutes, remove the pot from the heat. Serve immediately topped with the remaining Parmesan.

NOTE: To cut the basil into strips quickly, stack the leaves in a pile, then roll them into a long cylinder and slice thin.

# Linguine with Scallops

Scallops can be tricky to sauté unless you buy the right kind. It's important to search out "dry" scallops as opposed to the wet ones that are chemically treated to extend their shelf life. Dry scallops are unadulterated and will brown beautifully in the pan. They are also a bit more expensive and can be difficult to find, but it's worth the effort.

PREP TIME: 10 MINUTES
COOKING TIME: 10 MINUTES
SERVES 4

1 pound linguine
⅓ cup olive oil, or more if desired
2 medium garlic cloves, thinly sliced
1½ pounds sea scallops, sliced in half horizontally
¾ cup sun-dried tomatoes packed in oil, drained and cut into thin strips (see Note)
½ cup chopped fresh chives
½ teaspoon kosher salt
¼ teaspoon freshly ground black pepper
Freshly grated Parmesan cheese, for serving

Bring a large pot of lightly salted water to a boil over high heat. Add the linguine and cook until tender but still firm. (Tasting is the only way to know for sure.) Drain well and return to the pot.

While the linguine is cooking, heat the olive oil in a large sauté pan over medium-high heat. Add the garlic and stir briefly. Cook the scallops for 2 to 3 minutes without moving until cooked through, turning only once. Add the tomatoes, chives, salt, and pepper. Toss briefly to heat through.

Add the scallop mixture to the pasta and toss gently. Taste for salt and pepper. Transfer to bowls and sprinkle with generous amounts of Parmesan cheese.

NOTE: Many stores now have sun-dried tomatoes packed in oil that have already been cut into julienne strips. They cost a little more but are a tremendous time-saver.

# Simple, Perfect Spaghetti

Throughout the years, we've realized that the road to living what you love can be a winding one, with many twists and turns. Sometimes we all need to slow down, compose our thoughts, and start from scratch. There's something to be said for enjoying the simple things in life, especially when you feel like the world is spinning just a bit too fast. With only three ingredients, this pure, unadulterated recipe for spaghetti is truly one of the most comforting dishes we've come to enjoy.

PREP TIME: 10 MINUTES
COOKING TIME: 20 MINUTES
SERVES 4

1 pound spaghetti
½ cup (1 stick) unsalted butter, sliced thinly, at room temperature
1 cup shaved Parmigiano-Reggiano cheese, plus more for serving (see Note)
Kosher salt and freshly ground black pepper

Bring a large pot of lightly salted water to a boil over high heat. Add the pasta and cook until tender but still firm. (Tasting is the only way to know for sure.) Drain well.

While the spaghetti is cooking, put the butter into a large serving bowl. As soon as the pasta is done, add it to the bowl, top it with the cheese, and toss well to coat thoroughly. Taste for salt and pepper and serve immediately with extra Parmesan passed at the table.

NOTE: Use a swivel-type vegetable peeler to shave the Parmesan cheese. It gives you more texture than a grater.

## GODPARENTS

Sunday mornings in Anguilla are even more peaceful than other days. Families go to church, some by car and others by foot. In today's crazy world, we find it comforting to see men and women walking along the road with big hats shading them from the hot sun, holding Bibles and perhaps a tambourine if they happen to be in the choir.

We were honored when Lowell and Stacy asked us to be godparents to their new baby, but surprised when they said we were expected to stand up in front of the congregation at church. We hadn't realized that announcing our role as godparents was a public event to take place at little Zomahne's christening. Knowing we were nervous, Lowell said, "Don't worry. Once we're finished in church there's a big party at my brother's house."

Lowell's becoming a father was a major event at Blanchard's, and the whole staff was in church that day. T-shirts and baggy pants left behind, everyone looked ready to pose for a portrait in their Sunday finest. We were seated with the family and asked repeatedly if we were joining them for the reception

afterward. It slowly dawned on us that as important as this ceremony was, everyone was counting the minutes until the party.

We watched solemnly as the minister blessed Zoey and her parents. After several prayers and a selection of hymns, we were asked to stand and accept our appointment as godparents. Somehow, that responsibility seemed much more serious in church than when Lowell had first raised the subject at the restaurant. We gulped and then smiled at Zoey, knowing we had just started a new chapter in our life. We promised ourselves to be there for her whenever she needed a friend or guidance.

Every member of the Hodge family contributed something to eat at the reception. Food covered every inch of counter and tabletop throughout the house. There were hams, turkeys, chicken, ribs, fish prepared in at least five different ways, rice and peas, coleslaw, potato salad, green salad, baked yams, corn bread, baked beans, ice cream, cakes, pies, fruit salad, coconut tarts, and banana pudding.

Lowell's mom took us by the hand from room to room, introducing us to anyone we didn't already know. There were four generations of Hodges and though we loved meeting them all, we were more than a little confused by the end of the day. We had our picture taken holding Zoey so many times that our eyes were blinking nonstop from the flashes. By the time we got home that night, we marveled at how we felt after a day with the Hodges. We thought we were the ones doing the adopting and as it turned out, we'd just been adopted by a whole new family.

# Linguine with Clams

We make this often. It's quick, it's inexpensive, and everyone loves it. Our version produces a little extra sauce—almost like a broth—to be soaked up by a good loaf of bread. If company's coming, we'll toss in a dozen small fresh clams in the shell and steam them in the sauce before tossing with the pasta.

PREP TIME: 15 MINUTES
COOKING TIME: 10 MINUTES
SERVES 4

1 pound linguine
1/3 cup olive oil
6 small garlic cloves, thinly sliced
1/2 cup dry white wine
1/4 cup bottled clam juice
2 tablespoons fresh lemon juice
3 (6 1/2 ounce) cans chopped clams
12 littleneck or cherrystone clams (optional), scrubbed
1/3 cup chopped fresh parsley
Freshly ground black pepper
1/2 cup freshly grated Parmesan cheese

Bring a large pot of lightly salted water to a boil over high heat. Add the linguine and cook until tender but still firm. Drain well and return to the pot.

While the pasta is cooking, heat the oil in a large sauté pan over medium-high heat. When the oil is hot but not smoking, add the garlic and cook for 30 seconds. Add the wine, clam juice, lemon juice, and chopped clams with all of their juices. Bring to a boil and simmer for 5 minutes. (If you would like to add some fresh clams, this would be the time. Cover the pan and steam them for 5 minutes, or until they've all opened, discarding any that did not open.)

Pour the sauce over the linguine and toss well. Add the parsley and a generous grinding of pepper. Toss again, then transfer to bowls. Pass the Parmesan at the table.

# The Main Dish

* Grilled Steaks with Coconut and Lime
* Cabernet Chicken Stew
* Pan-Seared Sirloin with Shallot-Chive Butter
* Reggae Pork
* Veal Scaloppine with Marsala and Mustard
* Orange Pork Tenderloin
* Tequila Shrimp with Saffron Rice
* Roasted Thai Mussels
* Chicken Piccata
* Pan-Fried Mustard Chicken
* Moroccan Chicken
* Crusty Cheesy Cornmeal Chicken
* Lemon Roasted Chicken
* Roasted Salmon with Sesame Greens
* Grilled Swordfish with Cilantro and Lime
* Grilled Salmon with Chili-Ginger Aïoli

# distant flavors

When people ask what kind of food we like most, we immediately think of the flavors we've discovered away from home. We remember being in Bangkok with Jesse, and tasting the combination of coconut milk, lime, and ginger for the first time. It was in a simple neighborhood restaurant with not another tourist in sight. We were surrounded by businessmen negotiating deals over lunch and sophisticated Thai women with shopping bags piled high next to their seats. The scene was infused with pungent aromas, and we looked around curiously at bowls filled with food we hadn't yet been able to identify.

Our waitress helped us choose from the huge menu by pointing to what our neighbors were having. We watched them eat fat noodles with dark green leafy vegetables and shrimp with a sauce the color of mahogany, and we ordered accordingly. When we first tasted the sliced steak with ginger, lime, and coconut milk we were almost giddy. Sounds a little crazy, but that's what happens to us when we discover new foods. The excitement gets us all talking at once. "Mom, you have to serve this in the restaurant." Bob adds, "Let's have a Thai party when we get home and try to make this sauce."

As we explored beyond Bangkok, we found new and exotic flavors at regional markets throughout the country and in small family restaurants in hillside villages. The more memories we associated with these delicious new tastes, the more we wanted to duplicate them at home.

Food connects us with the rest of the world, near and far. When we bring home recipes from our travels, it fills our everyday life with more passion. When cooking and eating fill you with memories, the experience becomes much more meaningful.

Granted, our trip to Thailand was a once-in-a-lifetime extravagance, but it doesn't require an exotic locale to make an indelible food memory. In reality, many of the foods we enjoy come from ingredients and recipes we've gathered in our own backyard. Whether it's at the restaurant or at home, our best meals are the ones that come complete with stories. When we can share a memory about where we found a recipe or why we like a certain dish, the food inevitably tastes better.

# Grilled Steaks with Coconut and Lime

After tasting this combination of flavors in Thailand, we knew we had to try to re-create it at home. Each ingredient brings back another memory of our time in Bangkok and the incredible foods we discovered. Cooking what you love is about putting flavors together with experiences, so that every taste bud allows you to recollect a memory. Whether it's your honeymoon in Europe, the family vacation in the mountains, or a weekend camping trip, rediscovering moments through food can be just as rewarding as the trip itself.

PREP TIME: 5 MINUTES
COOKING TIME: 10 TO 12 MINUTES
SERVES 4

2 tablespoons fresh lime juice
½ cup unsweetened coconut milk
¼ cup heavy cream
½ tablespoon grated fresh lime peel
1½ tablespoons minced peeled fresh ginger
¾ teaspoon kosher salt, plus more for sprinkling (see Note)
4 sirloin steaks (12 ounces each)
Freshly ground black pepper

Prepare the grill or a ridged grill pan.

In a medium saucepan, whisk together the lime juice, coconut milk, cream, lime peel, ginger, and ¾ teaspoon salt. Heat until small bubbles form around the edge of the pan and set aside until the steaks are ready.

Sprinkle both sides of the steaks with a generous amount of salt and a fresh grinding of pepper. Grill over high heat to desired doneness, about 5 minutes on each side for medium-rare.

Reheat the sauce if needed and serve immediately with the steaks.

**NOTE:** We specify sprinkling kosher salt on the steaks before grilling because it creates a wonderful crust and seals in the juices.

# Cabernet Chicken Stew

Loosely based on a traditional recipe for coq au vin, this dish is unusual in that it also calls for red wine rather than white. It's delicious served over buttered noodles, rice, couscous, or anything simple that will absorb the sauce and soak up the flavor.

PREP TIME: 15 MINUTES
COOKING TIME: 1 HOUR
SERVES 4 TO 5

2 tablespoons olive oil, or more as needed
2 pounds boneless chicken breasts, cut into 2-inch pieces and patted dry
1 large yellow onion, cut in half and thinly sliced
½ pound carrots, cut into ½-inch slices
1 pound mushrooms, stemmed and quartered
1 cup chicken broth
½ cup Cabernet Sauvignon
¾ cup heavy cream
1 tablespoon fresh lemon juice
1 tablespoon Dijon mustard
1 teaspoon dried tarragon
1 teaspoon kosher salt
¼ teaspoon freshly ground black pepper

Preheat the oven to 375°F. Heat 2 tablespoons of the oil in a large ovenproof casserole over medium-high heat. Add the chicken and cook until golden brown on both sides, 5 to 6 minutes. If the size of your pot does not allow the chicken to cook in a single layer, it would be better to do this in two batches, combining them when the second batch is done.

Add the onion and mix it around with the chicken. Cook until the onion is almost soft and lightly browned, about 4 minutes. Add the carrots and cook another 2 minutes. Then add the mushrooms and cook 2 minutes longer.

Add the chicken broth, wine, cream, lemon juice, mustard, tarragon, salt, and pepper and mix well. Cover and bake for 45 minutes. Season with more salt and pepper to taste.

# Pan-Seared Sirloin with Shallot-Chive Butter

This recipe calls for thick steaks because it's much easier to cook them to the desired doneness than thin ones, which tend to overcook. If you prefer a smaller portion, just remember that sliced steak makes great leftovers. The steaks will continue to cook for several minutes after being removed from the pan so it's best to undercook them just slightly.

PREP TIME: 8 MINUTES
COOKING TIME: 10 MINUTES
SERVES 4

¼ cup (½ stick) unsalted butter, at room temperature
½ teaspoon balsamic vinegar
1 small shallot, minced
6 fresh chives, minced
¼ teaspoon kosher salt, plus more for seasoning (see Note)
¼ teaspoon freshly ground black pepper, plus more for seasoning
4 New York strip steaks (12 ounces each)
2 tablespoons olive oil

In a small bowl, use a fork to blend the butter, vinegar, shallot, chives, ¼ teaspoon salt, and ¼ teaspoon pepper. Set aside.

Season the steaks generously with salt and coarsely ground pepper on both sides. In a large sauté pan, heat the oil over medium-high heat until hot but not smoking. Cook the steaks for about 5 minutes on each side for medium-rare, turning only once. (Decrease or increase the cooking time if you prefer your meat more or less well done.)

Spread about a tablespoon of the butter over each steak and let rest in the pan for 2 minutes before serving.

**NOTE:** The coarse texture of the kosher salt helps form a delicious crust on the meat.

# Reggae Pork

Next time it's cold and gray outside and you need a shot of sunshine, give this a try. Put on some island music—Bob Marley or Jimmy Buffett works well—and make some Reggae Pork.

PREP TIME: 36 MINUTES (INCLUDING 30 MINUTES MARINATING TIME)
COOKING TIME: 6 MINUTES
SERVES 4

¼ cup fresh lime juice
¼ cup plus 2 tablespoons dark rum
¼ cup pineapple juice
1¼ pounds pork tenderloin, trimmed of fat and sliced ½ inch thick
8 ounces guava jelly
Kosher salt and freshly ground black pepper
Olive oil

In a medium bowl, whisk together the lime juice, ¼ cup rum, and the pineapple juice. Add the pork and marinate for 30 minutes to 1 hour. While the pork is marinating, warm the guava jelly and remaining 2 tablespoons of rum in a small saucepan. Remove from the heat and set aside.

Remove the pork from the marinade, pat until very dry with paper towels, and sprinkle with salt and pepper. Discard the marinade. In a large sauté pan, warm enough oil to cover the bottom of the pan over medium-high heat. Heat the oil until it is hot but not smoking. Cook the pork, turning only once, for 3 minutes on each side, or until cooked through and lightly browned.

Drizzle the pork with the warm guava jelly and rum mixture and serve immediately.

# Veal Scaloppine with Marsala and Mustard

There's something to be said for the energy of a noisy kitchen—dishes clanging, food sizzling, people singing. That's the atmosphere in the kitchen at our restaurant, making the preparation feel a little celebratory. Pounding out the veal slices adds to the moment. Here, we've taken an old standby and added whole-grain mustard, which gives some zest to the sweetness of the Marsala. The sauce also tastes great over noodles.

PREP TIME: 15 MINUTES
COOKING TIME: 12 MINUTES
SERVES 4

1 cup all-purpose flour
1 teaspoon kosher salt
½ teaspoon freshly ground black pepper
2 tablespoons olive oil
1½ pounds veal scaloppine, trimmed and pounded very thin
¾ cup Marsala wine
½ cup heavy cream
2 teaspoons whole-grain mustard
2 tablespoons chopped fresh parsley

Whisk together the flour, salt, and pepper in a shallow bowl. Heat the oil in a large sauté pan over medium-high heat until hot but not smoking. Dredge the veal on both sides in the flour, shaking off any excess. Quickly sauté in a single layer, about a minute on each side, transferring the cooked pieces to a plate as they are done.

Add the Marsala to the pan and stir, loosening the browned bits of veal with a whisk. On medium-low heat, cook for 2 minutes. Whisk in the cream and mustard and cook for 2 minutes more, or until slightly thickened.

Return the veal to the pan and turn the pieces to coat well with the sauce. Sprinkle with salt and pepper, garnish with parsley, and serve immediately.

# Orange Pork Tenderloin

Neither of us is crazy about marmalade. We've discovered, however, that using it as an ingredient in a recipe is remarkably different than slathering it on a piece of toast.

PREP TIME: 25 MINUTES (INCLUDING 20 MINUTES MARINATING TIME)
COOKING TIME: 10 MINUTES
SERVES 4

2 small garlic cloves, chopped
2 tablespoons balsamic vinegar
6 tablespoons olive oil
¼ cup orange juice
¼ cup soy sauce
1½ pounds pork tenderloin, trimmed and cut into ½-inch-thick slices

FOR THE SAUCE

2 teaspoons olive oil
2 small garlic cloves, chopped
1 teaspoon dried thyme leaves
3 tablespoons balsamic vinegar
⅔ cup good-quality orange marmalade

In a large bowl, make the marinade by whisking together the garlic, vinegar, 4 tablespoons of olive oil, orange juice, and soy sauce. Add the pork and coat well. Let sit at room temperature for 20 minutes.

While the pork is marinating, make the sauce. In a medium saucepan, heat the oil over medium heat. Add the garlic and thyme and stir for 30 seconds. Add the vinegar and marmalade and heat until warmed through. Set aside.

Place a thick layer of paper towels on the counter, remove the pork from the marinade, and dry thoroughly on the towels. Discard the marinade. In a large sauté pan, heat the remaining 2 tablespoons olive oil over high heat until hot but not smoking. Cook the pork in a single layer until browned, turning only once, 2 to 3 minutes on each side.

Arrange the pork on a serving platter and drizzle it with sauce.

# Tequila Shrimp with Saffron Rice

This variation on a classic paella is colorful and has tremendous depth of flavor—and the peppery sausage gives it a little kick. Our prep time includes preparing the shrimp but it's even faster if you buy shrimp that's been peeled and deveined.

PREP TIME: 20 MINUTES
COOKING TIME: 40 MINUTES
SERVES 6

¼ cup olive oil
5 medium garlic cloves, thinly sliced
1 large onion, chopped
1 large red bell pepper, chopped
½ pound chorizo (Spanish sausage), thinly sliced
3 large ripe tomatoes, chopped
1 (19-ounce) can black beans, drained
1½ cups tequila
1¼ cups chicken broth
1½ cups long-grain white rice
1 teaspoon kosher salt
1 large pinch saffron threads
¼ teaspoon turmeric
1½ pounds large shrimp, peeled and deveined

Preheat the oven to 400°F.

In a large, shallow ovenproof casserole or paella pan, heat the oil over medium heat. Add the garlic, onion, and bell pepper and cook for 4 minutes, stirring occasionally. Add the chorizo and cook for 1 minute. Add the tomatoes and beans and stir well. Increase the heat to high and add the tequila, chicken broth, rice, salt, saffron, and turmeric and stir well again. Cover and bring to a boil. Reduce the heat to medium and simmer for 10 minutes.

Add the shrimp, mix well, and bake uncovered for 15 minutes, or until the shrimp is cooked and the rice has absorbed the liquid.

SWEEP

# Roasted Thai Mussels

If you've never had roasted mussels, you have a wonderful treat in store. Add a salad and a loaf of crusty bread to soak up this intensely flavored Asian broth, and you've got a great meal fit for family or friends—and with minimal effort.

PREP TIME: 8 MINUTES
COOKING TIME: 10 MINUTES
SERVES 2

4 pounds mussels, well scrubbed and dried
1 cup unsweetened coconut milk
¼ cup chicken broth
¼ cup heavy cream
1½ tablespoons grated fresh lime peel
¼ cup fresh lime juice
3 tablespoons minced peeled fresh ginger
1½ teaspoons kosher salt
½ teaspoon freshly ground black pepper
⅓ cup fresh cilantro leaves

Preheat the oven to 500°F.

Arrange the mussels in a large roasting pan, making sure they cover the bottom. They can be piled in a double layer but any higher than that would prevent them from cooking evenly.

Combine the coconut milk, chicken broth, cream, lime peel, lime juice, ginger, salt, and pepper in a small bowl and pour over the mussels. Roast for 10 minutes, stirring occasionally, until all of the mussels have opened. Discard any that have not opened.

Transfer the mussels to shallow bowls and spoon the broth over the top. Scatter the cilantro over the mussels and serve immediately.

# Chicken Piccata

This dish is traditionally made with veal, but in real life, who really serves veal very often at home? We make this variation all the time, and, truthfully, the buttery lemon sauce and zing of the capers is just as delicious with chicken.

PREP TIME: 8 MINUTES
COOKING TIME: 10 MINUTES
SERVES 4

4 boneless, skinless chicken breast halves, patted dry (2½ to 3 pounds total)
Kosher salt and freshly ground black pepper
½ cup all-purpose flour
2 tablespoons olive oil
4 tablespoons (½ stick) unsalted butter
2 tablespoons fresh lemon juice
1 tablespoon capers, drained
2 tablespoons chopped fresh flat-leaf parsley

Cover the chicken breasts with a piece of plastic wrap and, using a meat pounder, flatten each breast to an even ¼-inch thickness. Sprinkle the chicken on both sides with salt and pepper. Put the flour in a shallow bowl. Dredge each piece of chicken in the flour and shake off any excess.

In a large sauté pan, heat the oil and 2 tablespoons of the butter over medium-high heat. When the foaming subsides, add the chicken and cook until golden brown on one side, 2 to 3 minutes. Turn the chicken and brown the other side, 1 to 2 minutes. When done, remove the chicken from the pan, sprinkle with a little more salt and pepper, and set aside.

Remove the pan from the heat and whisk in the lemon juice and capers, scraping up any brown bits and pieces left from the chicken. Whisk in the remaining 2 tablespoons of butter.

Return the chicken to the pan, turn the heat to medium, and heat for 1 minute. Garnish with parsley and serve immediately.

# Pan-Fried Mustard Chicken

Fried chicken is one of the great American comfort foods. We've made it easy to prepare by using boneless chicken breasts and have added some zesty flavor with two kinds of mustard. Our favorite way to serve this is topped with mixed lettuce that's been tossed with Caesar dressing. It makes a delicious one-dish dinner in no time at all.

PREP TIME: 15 MINUTES
COOKING TIME: 8 MINUTES
SERVES 4

3 tablespoons Dijon mustard
3 tablespoons whole-grain mustard
2 large egg yolks
3 tablespoons heavy cream
1 cup all-purpose flour
½ teaspoon kosher salt
¼ teaspoon freshly ground black pepper
1 cup dried bread crumbs, plain or Italian (see page 10)
4 boneless chicken breast halves, patted dry (2½ to 3 pounds total)
Olive oil, for sautéing

In a medium bowl, whisk together the mustards, egg yolks, and cream and set aside.

Place the flour, salt, and pepper in a shallow bowl and mix well. Place the bread crumbs in another shallow bowl and set aside.

Cover the chicken breasts with a piece of plastic wrap and, using a meat pounder, flatten each breast to an even ¼-inch thickness. Dredge each piece of chicken in the seasoned flour, shaking off any excess, then dip them into the mustard mixture and coat thoroughly. Finish by coating with the bread crumbs.

In a large sauté pan, heat enough olive oil to cover the bottom generously over medium-high heat. Cook the chicken, leaving it undisturbed, until golden brown on both sides and just cooked through, 3 to 4 minutes on each side.

# Moroccan Chicken

Even if you're not a big fan of apricots and prunes, we promise you won't be disappointed with this recipe. The fruits take on new flavor and texture when simmered with the chicken. Serve this with white rice to soak up the fragrant sauce.

PREP TIME: 10 MINUTES
COOKING TIME: 1 HOUR AND 10 MINUTES
SERVES 4 TO 5

3 tablespoons olive oil
2 garlic cloves, sliced thinly
1 large yellow onion, chopped
½ teaspoon ground ginger
½ teaspoon paprika
1 teaspoon turmeric
½ teaspoon ground cinnamon
1 cinnamon stick
Kosher salt and freshly ground black pepper
4 pounds chicken pieces on the bone (we use breasts and thighs)
2 cups dried apricot halves
2 cups prunes
2 tablespoons honey

In a large casserole, heat the oil over medium-high heat. Add the garlic and onion, and cook for 2 minutes, stirring often. Add the ginger, paprika, turmeric, ground cinnamon, and cinnamon stick. Sprinkle with salt and pepper and stir well. Add the chicken and enough water to almost cover.

Cover the pot and bring to a boil over high heat. Reduce the heat and simmer, partially covered, for 45 minutes. Add the apricots, prunes, and honey and simmer for 15 minutes more, or until the fruit is soft and the chicken is cooked through.

# Crusty Cheesy Cornmeal Chicken

We're always looking for recipes that are simple, quick, and loaded with flavor. This one includes one of our favorite cheeses—herby French Boursin—and mixes it with the unexpected kick of chili powder. Dinner can be ready in less than half an hour—just butter some noodles, toss mixed greens with your favorite dressing, and you're done!

PREP TIME: 9 MINUTES
COOKING TIME: 20 MINUTES
SERVES 6

1 cup chicken broth
1 cup dry white wine
12 ounces Boursin cheese
4 boneless chicken breast halves (2½ to 3 pounds total)
2½ cups yellow cornmeal, coarse variety if available
2 teaspoons kosher salt
¾ teaspoon freshly ground black pepper
1 teaspoon chili powder
4 large eggs
Olive oil, for sautéing

In a large saucepan, combine the chicken broth and wine and bring to a boil over high heat. Continue to boil vigorously until it is reduced to about ½ cup, about 10 minutes. Reduce the heat to low and whisk in the Boursin until smooth. Remove from the heat.

Cut the chicken breasts in half crosswise. Holding your knife parallel to the cutting board, slice the thicker half of each breast horizontally so you end up with a total of 12 thin chicken cutlets.

Place the cornmeal, salt, pepper, and chili powder in a shallow bowl and mix well. In another shallow bowl, beat the eggs. Coat the chicken with the cornmeal mixture, shaking off any excess. Dip each piece in the egg and finish with a second coating of the cornmeal mixture.

In a large sauté pan, heat enough olive oil to lightly cover the bottom over

medium-high heat until hot but not smoking. Cook the chicken, leaving it undisturbed and turning it only once, about 3 minutes on each side. It should be golden brown and cooked through. If the pan becomes dry and starts to smoke, lower the heat slightly and add a little more oil.

Warm the sauce if necessary and serve immediately with the chicken.

# Lemon Roasted Chicken

Family traditions are such treasures. When Bob was growing up in Vermont, his family had roasted chicken for dinner every Sunday. This recipe is based on that Blanchard family standby. Adding lemons really brightens and freshens the final dish. And if you're making one roasted chicken, you may as well make two—it takes the same amount of time and you're guaranteed leftovers for the next few days.

PREP TIME: 10 MINUTES
COOKING TIME: 1¼ TO 1½ HOURS
SERVES 8 TO 10

2 roasting chickens (4½ to 5 pounds each)
6 tablespoons (¾ stick) unsalted butter
2 tablespoons fresh lemon juice
½ teaspoon kosher salt
½ teaspoon freshly ground black pepper
6 fresh rosemary sprigs
6 medium shallots, peeled and cut in half
3 lemons, quartered
10 small red potatoes
2 large sweet onions, thickly sliced
6 carrots, cut into 2-inch lengths
4 parsnips, cut into 2-inch lengths
3 tablespoons olive oil

Preheat the oven to 400°F. Remove the giblets and rinse the birds inside and out. Pat dry with paper towels.

In a small saucepan, melt the butter with the lemon juice, salt, and pepper over low heat. Place the chickens on a rack in a large roasting pan and stuff each with 3 sprigs of rosemary, 6 shallot halves, and 6 lemon quarters.

Rub the lemon-butter thoroughly over the outside of the chickens. Tie the legs together with kitchen twine.

In a large bowl, toss the potatoes, onions, carrots, and parsnips with the olive oil and a sprinkling of salt and pepper. Arrange the vegetables around the chickens and roast for $1^{1}/_{4}$ to $1^{1}/_{2}$ hours, or until a meat thermometer registers 170° F when inserted into the thickest part of the thigh. The juices should run clear when you insert a knife between a leg and a thigh.

## DINNER FOR THE SKI TEAM

We're a skiing family. In New England, that's pretty common. But our son, Jesse, was so in love with the thrill of flying down a mountain that his passion led him to the junior racing circuit. Whether it's ballet, piano, gymnastics, hockey, soccer, horseback riding, skating, or skiing, any parent knows what it takes to keep up the pace of competitive sports: training after school, competitions on weekends, specialized summer camp, and more money than anyone will ever dare to admit.

And when this investment of time and energy pays off, it deserves recognition. Our kids should know we're proud of their dedication and hard work. They should feel we've lived through their ups and downs and have supported them every step of the way.

When Jesse qualified for the Junior Olympics, it was definitely time to celebrate. Since our house was the closest to the mountain, the whole team spent the weekend with us. Weeks before everyone arrived, we knew dinner was going to be a challenge. We wanted to celebrate this landmark event with a special meal, but we needed to serve food that teenagers would eat. This was not an easy undertaking. We just couldn't bear to make the usual lasagne or spaghetti. Our first thought was to make a fun Mexican dinner or maybe even Indian. But we couldn't risk using exotic spices and having kids go hungry.

Finally, it came to us. We stuffed six chickens with lemons, shallots, and rosemary; surrounded them with plenty of potatoes and carrots; and roasted them until crispy and golden brown. Presenting the birds on large carving platters, we were received with oooohs and wows that we knew a pan of lasagne would never have produced.

Years later, when we opened the restaurant, we observed a strange phenomenon among the parents of young children. When ready to order, many tell us that their children have specific food requirements. "A plain bowl of pasta," they'll say, "with a little butter and Parmesan cheese on the side. Unless you have chicken fingers and French fries. That would be even better."

We can't help but wonder when this monotonous and bland menu became standard fare for the under-twelve set. We know from experience that children savor the tangy flavor of lemon and the intoxicating aroma of the rosemary as much as we do. Why is it that parents feel they need to shield their kids from these exciting flavors? Instead, they actually encourage the pasta-and-chicken-finger syndrome by announcing to the world that it is all their children will accept for dinner. Very odd, don't you think?

# Roasted Salmon with Sesame Greens

Roasting salmon fillets is so easy. It requires minimal attention and the fish doesn't dry out as it often can on the grill. The Asian flavors in this recipe complement the salmon perfectly.

PREP TIME: 10 MINUTES
COOKING TIME: 12 MINUTES
SERVES 4

¼ cup rice wine vinegar
1 teaspoon soy sauce
1 small garlic clove, minced
2 teaspoons minced peeled fresh ginger
¼ cup tahini (sesame paste), stirred well
3 tablespoons olive oil
4 thick salmon fillets (6 to 7 ounces each)
Kosher salt and freshly ground black pepper
6 cups mixed baby greens, washed and dried well

Preheat the oven to 475°F.

In a small bowl, whisk together the vinegar, soy sauce, garlic, ginger, tahini, and 2 tablespoons water until blended. Set aside.

Coat a small sheet pan with 1 tablespoon of the oil. Coat the salmon on all sides with the remaining olive oil and sprinkle with salt and pepper. Roast until just done, 10 to 12 minutes for 1-inch fillets.

While the salmon is in the oven, toss the greens with just enough dressing to coat. Divide the salad onto four plates and top with the salmon when ready. Serve immediately.

# Grilled Swordfish with Cilantro and Lime

Swordfish is available year-round and there's no reason to limit the grilling season to the summer months. Invest in a good-quality, cast-iron stovetop grill pan and it can be July all year. We like the kind that spans two burners and has ridges on one side and a smooth griddle for sandwiches and pancakes on the other.

PREP TIME: 10 MINUTES
COOKING TIME: 10 MINUTES
SERVES 4

2 tablespoons unsalted butter, at room temperature
2 tablespoons unsweetened coconut milk
1 tablespoon fresh lime juice
1 small shallot, minced
1 ½ tablespoons finely chopped fresh cilantro
Kosher salt and freshly ground black pepper
4 swordfish steaks (8 ounces each)
2 tablespoons olive oil

Preheat an indoor grill pan or outdoor grill.

Using a fork, mash together the butter, coconut milk, lime juice, shallot, cilantro, and ¼ teaspoon each of salt and pepper. Set aside.

Brush the swordfish with olive oil and sprinkle with salt and pepper on both sides.

Grill the steaks, turning only once, for about 5 minutes on each side, or until cooked through.

Spread about a tablespoon of the butter mixture over each piece of fish and let rest for 2 minutes before serving.

# Grilled Salmon with Chili-Ginger Aïoli

Aïoli is typically loaded with garlic, but for some dishes we prefer softer, more delicate flavors. In this nontraditional version, we've replaced the garlic with a wonderfully aromatic combination of flavors. Top the hot fillets with a generous spoonful as soon as they come off the grill so the aïoli can melt into the fish.

PREP TIME: 12 MINUTES
COOKING TIME: 10 MINUTES
SERVES 4

FOR THE AÏOLI

1 cup Hellmann's mayonnaise
½ teaspoon grated fresh lime peel
1 tablespoon fresh lime juice
1 tablespoon minced peeled fresh ginger
1½ teaspoons Worcestershire sauce
1½ teaspoons Asian chili sauce, sweet or spicy as desired
2 teaspoons minced fresh cilantro

FOR THE SALMON

4 (1-inch-thick) salmon fillets (6 to 7 ounces each)
3 tablespoons olive oil
Kosher salt and freshly ground black pepper

Preheat an indoor grill pan or outdoor grill to medium-high heat.

Make the aïoli: Whisk all the ingredients together in a small bowl and set aside.

Make the salmon: Brush the fish on both sides with the oil and sprinkle lightly with salt and pepper.

Grill the fillets just until opaque in the center, 4 to 5 minutes on each side. Top each with a dollop of aïoli and pass what's left at the table.

# Vegetables and Sides

* Parmesan Ditalini
* Old-Fashioned Creamed Corn
* Grilled Lemons
* Coconut Rice
* Sautéed Corn and Snow Peas
* Roasted Asparagus
* Mexican Mashed Potatoes
* Red Pepper–Mozzarella "Sandwiches"
* Grilled Corn
* Potato-Artichoke Gratin
* Grilled Cinnamon Bananas
* Roasted Wild Mushrooms
* Crispy Grilled Quesadillas
* Noodles with Green Peppercorns
* Garlic Bread

# grapes, grapes, and more grapes

We buy much of our wine for the restaurant directly from vineyards in France. Not only does it give us a better selection than we could get through distributors, but we enjoy numerous visits to the French countryside, meeting vintners and tasting wine. Several years ago we invited Lowell, our manager, and Miguel, our wine steward, to join us on one of our pilgrimages. We've traveled since quite a bit together, but this was one of their first trips beyond the Caribbean islands.

We picked up a sporty little Volvo at Charles de Gaulle airport, and the four of us headed off for Reims to visit several Champagne suppliers. As we zoomed along the A4, Lowell and Miguel stared out the windows at the expansive farms that cover the region northeast of Paris. Immense flat fields of sunflowers and corn seemed to go on forever. "Anguilla is so dry," Miguel said. "We could never grow all this stuff." And as we traveled farther and farther away from the city, both Lowell and Miguel commented not only on the farms but also on the immense distances between towns. "We could have driven the length of Anguilla ten times by now," Lowell said in amazement.

The level fields gradually gave way to rolling hills, and as we worked our way over the small mountain range outside of Reims, we spotted our first vineyard. Shy Miguel was so excited he could hardly contain himself. Lowell looked incredulously at the passing scenery and said, "Man, this the real thing now." We were in the heart of quintessential France and it was beautiful. There wasn't a soul in sight; just grapevines everywhere we looked.

We pulled off the road and walked over to the edge of a field. Long, orderly rows of vines rolled down into the valley, up and over the hills, and out of sight. It was September and almost harvest time. Lowell and Miguel each picked a large bunch of the juicy pinot noir grapes, and we took pictures as they popped them reverently into their mouths.

After tasting Champagnes and touring the extensive underground cellars of Reims, we drove down through the bright yellow mustard fields of Dijon and into Burgundy. We sampled beef bourguignon, coq au vin, and more wines than any of us can remember. Miguel and Lowell came home dreaming of escargots and chocolate soufflés, neither of which are standard fare in Anguilla. The following year, Clinton, our sous chef, got his hands on a French cookbook and made Miguel a chocolate soufflé for his birthday. We were touched by the thoughtful gesture and vowed to have Clinton join us on our next buying trip to France.

# Parmesan Ditalini

It's amazing how just a few simple ingredients can be combined to make something understated but spectacular. Ditalini pasta is typically used in soups because of its small size. Its tiny, tubular shape also makes it great for a side dish; we love it with baby peas and shavings of fresh Parmesan. Use a vegetable peeler to make the Parmesan shavings.

PREP TIME: 5 MINUTES
COOKING TIME: 10 MINUTES
SERVES 4

1 ½ cups ditalini pasta
2 tablespoons unsalted butter, at room temperature
1 cup baby frozen green peas, thawed under cool running water
Kosher salt and freshly ground black pepper
½ cup Parmesan cheese shavings (2 ounces)

Bring a large pot of lightly salted water to a boil over high heat. Add the ditalini and cook until tender but still firm. (Tasting is the only way to know for sure.) Drain well and return to the pot.

Add the butter and peas to the ditalini and stir well over a low heat until the peas are heated through, about 1 minute. Season with salt and pepper to taste.

Transfer the ditalini to a serving bowl, top with the Parmesan shavings, and serve immediately.

# Old-Fashioned Creamed Corn

It's so satisfying to take a recipe that most people associate with a can and make the real thing from scratch at home. This corn is incredibly rich and creamy—and so easy to make. It's a perfect accompaniment to simple grilled chicken or steak because it eliminates the need for any additional sauce.

PREP TIME: 7 MINUTES
COOKING TIME: 12 MINUTES
SERVES 4

2 cups (1 10-ounce package) frozen corn kernels (see Note)
¼ cup milk
2 tablespoons unsalted butter
1 ¼ cups heavy cream
1 tablespoon fresh lemon juice
¼ teaspoon kosher salt
⅛ teaspoon freshly ground black pepper

In a food processor, puree 1 cup of the corn with the milk.

In a large sauté pan, melt the butter over medium-high heat. Add the pureed corn, the remaining corn kernels, and the cream, lemon juice, salt, and pepper. Bring to a boil. Reduce the heat and simmer uncovered for 5 minutes, or until creamy and thickened. Season with salt and pepper to taste.

NOTE: This recipe can be made with fresh or frozen corn, depending on the time of year. If using fresh, you'll need about 4 ears to yield 2 cups of corn. If using frozen, look for Birds Eye Deluxe Tender Sweet Corn, thaw in a colander under cool running water, and dry well with paper towels.

# Grilled Lemons

Experiencing food is more than just savoring the delicious flavors—it's also about the rich colors, scents, and textures that appeal to our other senses. We often throw a few lemons on the grill when we cook swordfish, shrimp, or any kind of seafood. At the restaurant, we serve them with grilled lobster. They add an aesthetic touch to the table, and the warm juice practically pours out of the skin with the slightest squeeze.

PREP TIME: 1 MINUTE
COOKING TIME: 5 MINUTES
MAKES 8 HALVES

4 lemons

Preheat a grill or grill pan. Cut the lemons in half crosswise and grill cut side down until they are golden brown. Serve while still warm.

# Coconut Rice

Rice is an essential dish in many cultures, including the Caribbean. It's extremely versatile and can be prepared in a multitude of ways. Though everyone starts out with the same tiny grain, it can be transformed into a unique creation based on our own traditions and tastes. This version is a longtime Blanchard's favorite.

PREP TIME: 4 MINUTES
COOKING TIME: 20 MINUTES
SERVES 6

1 cup jasmine rice
1 cup unsweetened coconut milk, well shaken
2 teaspoons grated fresh lime peel
1 tablespoon fresh lime juice
1 teaspoon kosher salt
¼ teaspoon freshly ground black pepper

Combine all of the ingredients with 1½ cups water in a medium saucepan over high heat. Cover and bring to a boil. Reduce the heat to low and simmer for 20 minutes, or until all of the liquid is absorbed.

# Sautéed Corn and Snow Peas

It's not just the beautiful yellow and green colors that we love about this dish. It's versatile, easy, and has a wonderful combination of textures. The snow peas and corn are a little crunchy and taste fresh and summery.

PREP TIME: 12 MINUTES
COOKING TIME: 8 MINUTES
SERVES 4

4 ears corn, shucked
2 tablespoons unsalted butter
2 tablespoons minced peeled fresh ginger
2 large shallots, chopped
½ pound snow peas, trimmed and cut crosswise into ¼-inch strips
½ teaspoon kosher salt
⅛ teaspoon freshly ground black pepper
1 tablespoon fresh lime juice

Using a sharp knife, cut the kernels off the cobs.

Melt the butter in a medium sauté pan over medium heat. Add the ginger and shallots, and cook until almost soft, 2 to 3 minutes. Add the corn, snow peas, salt, and pepper and cook until just tender, 5 to 6 minutes, stirring often.

Stir in the lime juice, add more salt and pepper to taste, and serve.

# Roasted Asparagus

It's not by chance that we prepare certain foods the way we do. When it comes to asparagus, there's no comparison between roasted and steamed. Roasting is just as easy, but it gives the spears a deeper flavor and much more texture.

PREP TIME: 7 MINUTES
COOKING TIME: 10 MINUTES
SERVES 4 TO 6

2 pounds asparagus, trimmed
1 tablespoon olive oil
Kosher salt and freshly ground black pepper
3 tablespoons unsalted butter
1 large garlic clove, minced
2 teaspoons grated fresh lemon peel
2 tablespoons fresh lemon juice

Preheat the oven to 400°F. Line a sheet pan with parchment paper.

Place the asparagus on the sheet pan, toss with the olive oil, and arrange in a single layer. Sprinkle with salt and pepper and roast until tender, 8 to 10 minutes, depending on size.

In a large sauté pan, melt the butter over medium-high heat. As soon as the butter stops foaming, add the garlic and lemon peel, and cook for 1 minute. Add the asparagus and lemon juice, and toss together to coat well. Sprinkle with salt and pepper and serve.

# Mexican Mashed Potatoes

We like our mashed potatoes smooth. This recipe calls for canned chiles instead of fresh, which are softer in texture and don't interfere with the creamy potatoes.

PREP TIME: 12 MINUTES
COOKING TIME: 30 MINUTES
SERVES 4

1 ½ pounds baking potatoes, peeled and cut into 1-inch pieces
Kosher salt and freshly ground black pepper
½ cup milk
¼ cup (½ stick) unsalted butter, at room temperature
1 cup shredded sharp white Cheddar cheese (4 ounces)
½ cup diced canned green chiles, mild or spicy
2 tablespoons coarsely chopped fresh cilantro

Place the potatoes in a large pot and cover with water. Add a few pinches of salt and bring to a boil. Uncover and cook until the potatoes are tender, about 15 minutes. Drain and return the potatoes to the pot. Add the milk and butter, and mash well with a fork or potato masher.

Stir in the cheese, chiles, and cilantro. Season with salt and pepper to taste.

# Red Pepper–Mozzarella "Sandwiches"

Who says a sandwich has to include bread? This recipe was inspired by some of our favorite antipasti platters at Tuscan trattorias. When the mozzarella melts between the two pieces of red pepper, the contrast of texture is remarkable. These are not complicated to make but unusual enough to get rave reviews.

PREP TIME: 5 MINUTES
COOKING TIME: 20 MINUTES
SERVES 4

¼ cup olive oil
2 tablespoons balsamic vinegar
4 medium red bell peppers
8 large fresh basil leaves
4 ounces fresh mozzarella cheese, thinly sliced
Kosher salt and freshly ground black pepper
¼ cup freshly grated Parmesan cheese

Prepare a grill or preheat the oven to 450°F.

In a small bowl, combine 2 tablespoons of the oil with the vinegar and set aside. Cut both ends off the peppers and discard or reserve for another use. Cut the peppers in half lengthwise, and remove the seeds and the white ribs.

Coat the peppers with the remaining 2 tablespoons of oil and cook until soft. If using the oven, bake them on a sheet pan lined with parchment paper for 10 to 15 minutes, or until soft. If grilling, cook over medium heat for another 5 to 10 minutes, or until soft.

When the peppers are cooked, place them skin side down and put 2 basil leaves on 4 of the pepper halves. Arrange the mozzarella on top of the basil and season liberally with salt and pepper. Sprinkle each with a tablespoon of Parmesan and cover with the remaining pepper halves, skin side up.

Bake or grill the sandwiches until the cheese is slightly melted, 2 to 3 minutes. Drizzle the reserved oil and vinegar mixture over the top and serve immediately.

# Grilled Corn

Some people husk their corn before grilling it. Though we love the grilled flavor, we've found that husking the corn first dries it out. We recommend removing the silk but leaving the husk loosely attached, which helps keep the corn moist and still gives you that great grilled flavor.

PREP TIME: 10 MINUTES
COOKING TIME: 6 MINUTES
SERVES 6

6 ears corn, with husks
Unsalted butter, at room temperature
Kosher salt and freshly ground black pepper

Prepare a grill or place a grill pan over medium heat on the stove.

Remove the outermost layer of the husks. Pull back the remaining husks just enough so you can remove the silk. Loosely recover the corn with the husks, leaving some of the kernels exposed, which will allow them to brown slightly. Grill the corn for 5 to 6 minutes, turning frequently until tender and heated through.

Serve immediately with butter, salt, and pepper.

# Potato-Artichoke Gratin

We find that some gratins can be dry and bland. The secret to this version is the Gruyère, which gives it a great rich, cheesy texture. It makes a large quantity, but don't worry—it's just as good the next day.

PREP TIME: 15 MINUTES
COOKING TIME: 1 HOUR
SERVES 8

1 (14-ounce) can artichoke hearts, drained well
2 tablespoons unsalted butter
1 medium onion, thinly sliced
2 pounds baking potatoes, peeled
8 ounces Gruyère cheese, shredded (2 cups)
2 cups plus 2 tablespoons heavy cream
1 ½ teaspoons kosher salt
¼ teaspoon freshly ground black pepper

Preheat the oven to 375°F. Butter a shallow 10-cup baking dish. Cut the artichokes in quarters lengthwise.

In a medium sauté pan, heat the butter over medium-high heat. Add the onion and cook for 10 minutes or until tender.

Slice the potatoes very thin and place them in a large bowl. Add 1½ cups of the Gruyère along with 2 cups of the cream, the salt, pepper, and onion. Mix well. Place half of the potatoes in the baking dish and arrange the artichokes over the top. Cover with the remaining potatoes.

In a small bowl, combine the remaining ½ cup of Gruyère with the remaining 2 tablespoons cream and sprinkle over the potatoes. Bake for 1 hour, or until well browned and bubbling. Allow to set for 10 minutes before serving.

# Grilled Cinnamon Bananas

These sweet glazed bananas make a great accompaniment to spicy foods. In the restaurant we serve them every night with our hot Jamaican jerk shrimp, a powerful, spicy dish that has become one of our most popular items. Try to find firm, just ripe bananas. If they're too green, a bitter taste will come through. If they're too soft, they won't hold up on the grill.

PREP TIME: 5 MINUTES
COOKING TIME: 10 MINUTES
SERVES 8

2 tablespoons unsalted butter
¼ cup molasses
1 teaspoon Myers dark rum
1 teaspoon ground cinnamon
1 tablespoon honey
4 ripe, firm bananas

Prepare an outdoor grill or heat a grill pan over medium-high heat on the stove.

Place all the ingredients except the bananas in a medium saucepan and cook over a very low heat just until combined. Cut the bananas in half lengthwise, leaving the peels on. Brush the glaze on the cut side of the banana halves and place skin side down on the grill.

Cook until soft, about 8 minutes. Using tongs, carefully turn the bananas over and cook for 1 to 2 minutes on the cut side. Serve immediately, glazed side up.

# Roasted Wild Mushrooms

We've suggested using three types of mushrooms for a good combination of color and texture. This is a mix we like, but feel free to substitute other varieties. If you use oyster mushrooms, they will probably come in a very large bunch. Just cut them into manageable clumps and keep some of the stem attached to each so they don't break apart into little pieces.

PREP TIME: 10 MINUTES
COOKING TIME: 15 MINUTES
SERVES 4

6 ounces shiitake mushrooms
6 ounces chanterelle mushrooms
6 ounces oyster mushrooms
⅓ cup olive oil
Kosher salt and freshly ground black pepper

Preheat the oven to 425°F. Line a sheet pan with parchment paper.

Remove the stems from the mushrooms and discard. Place the mushrooms on the sheet pan and toss with the olive oil. Sprinkle with salt and pepper.

Roast for 15 minutes, or until tender when pierced with a fork.

# Crispy Grilled Quesadillas

One of our favorite experiences on our trips to Mexico is eating freshly made tortillas. While most quesadilla recipes call for flour tortillas, we prefer the crispier, heartier results that come from using corn. Just put these on the grill alongside steaks or chicken and you needn't bother with another more elaborate side dish from inside the kitchen.

PREP TIME: 10 MINUTES
COOKING TIME: 6 MINUTES
SERVES 6

8 (6-inch) corn tortillas
Olive oil
2 tablespoons prepared barbecue sauce
½ cup roasted red peppers from a jar, drained well and cut into strips
1 ¼ cups shredded Monterey Jack cheese
⅓ cup freshly grated Parmesan cheese
2 tablespoons chopped cilantro
5 scallions, thinly sliced (green and white parts)

Prepare the grill. Brush one side of each tortilla with olive oil.

Place 4 of the tortillas oil side down on a cutting board and spread the barbecue sauce evenly over each. Arrange the peppers over the tortillas. Sprinkle on the cheeses, and scatter the cilantro and scallions over the top. Cover each with the remaining 4 tortillas, oil side up, and press gently.

Carry the quesadillas to the grill right on the cutting board. Carefully transfer them to the grill and cook for 3 minutes, or until the bottom is slightly crisped and golden brown. Using a spatula, carefully flip the quesadillas and cook for another 3 minutes, or until the cheese is melted and the bottom begins to get crispy.

Transfer them back to the cutting board, cut each into six wedges, and serve immediately.

# BLANCHARD'S SPORTS CLUB

If we close our eyes and imagine the kind of people we'd most like to spend time with, a picture of our staff would unquestionably materialize. Not only do we work well together and manage to have fun at the same time, but we are proud to know them outside of the restaurant as well. Several years ago they formed a group called the Blanchard's Sports Club. They sponsor and organize boat races, disco nights, barbecues, concerts, and most notably bike races. One of their most popular events is an annual charity bike race with competitors from all over the Caribbean.

Ozzie is the group leader when it comes to organizing these events, and his spirit is endless; he can do so many things at once it's mind-boggling. (His nickname is "Motion," which should give you an idea of his energy level.) He plans the bike races down to the last detail. "Sugar" the D.J. is hired to provide entertainment for the crowd, and police are positioned along the route to control traffic. Miguel and Rinso buy cases of Heineken and other drinks for the bar, and Ozzie loads up on chicken and ribs to sell to spectators.

Blanchard's is home base where the race starts and finishes. Ozzie, Bug, Lowell, and Alex set up tents to shade the two grills, the bar, and Sugar's wall of speakers. Clinton and Garrilin start baking the chicken and ribs at six in the morning so all they have to do is finish them off on the grill during the race. Miguel is the only Blanchard's member that actually enters the race, so he spends the morning stretching and psyching himself up for the competition.

When the race begins, Ozzie leads the pack on a Vespa scooter followed by the riders and a procession of cars, motorcycles, and pickups filled with fans showing their support. Once the

start signal sounds and the racers are out of sight, business intensifies under the tents. Bug and Hughes man the grills, Tarah and Mel sell the food, and Rinso and I handle the bar. Clinton, Alex, Garrilin, Alfonso, and Lowell keep us stocked with whatever we need from the restaurant. It's a steady relay all day long.

The race starts with a ten-mile stretch into town and back to the restaurant again. Then they do twelve three-mile laps around the salt pond, passing hundreds of enthusiastic fans in front of the restaurant each time they go around. With every lap, the cheering and thumping of the music rise several decibels, reaching a deafening crescendo as the winner crosses the finish line.

Ozzie officiates at the awards ceremony, handing out trophies and cash prizes to the top five. He then exuberantly announces that the club will be donating half of the proceeds to a school charity that sends deserving students off island for further education. We look on while the crowd roars with approval.

Last year he topped the presentation off with one more announcement. He motioned for the entire staff to step up to the podium and positioned us in the foreground. In front of an embarrassingly large group of Anguillans and tourists, we were presented with a glass plaque engraved with the words "To the Best Bosses Ever." Covered with barbecue sauce and spilled Heineken, we cried and hugged them all.

# Noodles with Green Peppercorns

Sometimes simple is better. Over the years, we've found that some of the tastiest recipes are often the easiest to make. Crunchy peppercorns are a great way to liven up this side dish and give the noodles a slightly spicy flavor that is pleasantly surprising. Add more if you want to turn up the heat.

PREP TIME: 10 MINUTES
COOKING TIME: 6 MINUTES
SERVES 6

½ pound broad egg noodles
1 tablespoon green peppercorns packed in brine, drained
¼ cup (½ stick) unsalted butter, cut into small pieces
½ teaspoon kosher salt

Bring a large pot of lightly salted water to a boil over high heat. Add the noodles and cook until tender but still firm. (Tasting is the only way to know for sure.) Drain well and return to the pot.

While the noodles are cooking, finely chop the peppercorns. Toss the noodles with the butter, peppercorns, and salt, and serve immediately.

# Garlic Bread

We used to think garlic bread belonged only with an Italian dinner, but now we often put some on the grill at summer barbecues. During the colder months, it can be cooked on a stovetop grill, making it easy to enjoy all year long. Sourdough bread is perfect for this recipe, but any crusty loaf will work just fine. Olive bread adds even more flavor and texture.

PREP TIME: 3 MINUTES
COOKING TIME: 5 MINUTES
SERVES 4

2 tablespoons olive oil or melted unsalted butter
4 thick slices hearty rustic bread
1 large garlic clove, peeled and cut in half

Brush a little of the oil or butter on both sides of the bread. Brown lightly on both sides on an outdoor grill, stovetop grill pan, or broiler. Rub one side of each slice of bread with a cut side of the garlic clove and serve immediately.

# Desserts

* Extra Lemony Lemon Squares
* Baked Peaches and Cinnamon Cream
* No-Name Dessert
* Key Lime Pie in a Glass
* Pumpkin Whoopie Pies
* Chocolate Croissant Pudding
* S'mores
* Chocolate Icebox Cakes with Coffee Cream
* Chocolate Chip Oatmeal Cookies
* Key Lime Pound Cake

# parties and campfires

**Do you remember** how it felt as a kid to sit around a campfire? Faces glowed and shadows danced as the crackle of wood connected you to the

people around the circle. You told stories and shared dreams. Those memories and friendships seemed like they'd last forever. And more often than not, food was part of the reason to gather everyone together: roasting hot dogs on the end of a stick you found in the woods, shaking popcorn over the coals or making our all-time favorite—S'mores.

Good parties are about creating memories. When we built our house, we knew we wanted plenty of outside space for entertaining. We planned the barbecue

area, the dining table on our stone patio surrounded by birch trees, and a back porch for drinks and hors d'oeuvres. But our favorite place is one that was the easiest to create and required only a little imagination.

Beyond our backyard is a clearing in the woods where the ground is blanketed with ferns. It's such a beautiful area and we wanted to think of a way to share it with our friends. As soon as we came up with the idea of building a campfire circle, we knew it was perfect. Cooking together in such a dreamy setting would give us memorable evenings for years to come.

We cleared a path through the ferns, covered it with bark chips, and opened up a circular area bordered by maple trees. We found a giant old brass kettle at a flea market to hold the fire itself, and surrounded it with Adirondack chairs. It's been such a success that when friends come for dinner, they would be disappointed if we didn't end up making S'mores, telling stories, and stargazing behind the house.

Since then, we've seen numerous ways to create campfires in a backyard. Mail-order catalogues and garden centers sell various types of firepits, some complete with barbecue grills for more elaborate cooking. Even an old kettle grill with its legs removed works beautifully. We've included the recipe for S'mores here, knowing full well you already know how to make them. But we hope it will remind you how much fun they really are.

# Extra Lemony Lemon Squares

We've always savored the flavor of lemon and call for a bit of lemon juice in many of our recipes. This dessert celebrates this delicious, tart fruit with tremendous flavor in each bite. They are as lemony as can be. When we pile them on a platter for friends at home, they're gone in no time.

PREP TIME: 15 MINUTES
COOKING TIME: 35 MINUTES
MAKES 24

2¼ cups all-purpose flour
½ cup confectioners' sugar, plus extra for sprinkling
1 cup (2 sticks) cold unsalted butter, cut into small cubes
2 cups granulated sugar
½ teaspoon baking powder
4 large eggs
1 tablespoon grated fresh lemon peel
½ cup fresh lemon juice

Preheat the oven to 350°F.

In a large bowl, sift together 2 cups of the flour and the confectioners' sugar. Using your fingers or a pastry blender, cut in the butter until the mixture is coarse and crumbly. Press the mixture evenly into a 9 × 13-inch baking pan, working the dough about ½ inch up the sides. Bake for 20 minutes.

In a large mixing bowl, whisk together the granulated sugar, remaining ¼ cup flour, the baking powder, eggs, lemon peel, and lemon juice. Pour over the crust and bake for 15 minutes, or until set in the center.

Allow to cool before dusting with confectioners' sugar and cutting into squares.

## WINTER IN VERMONT

We spend 99 percent of the winter months in Anguilla, where it's 82 degrees and sunny almost every day. The turquoise sea splashes up on the white sandy shore outside our windows and our restaurant is filled with people escaping the cold.

Cooking what we love in Anguilla usually means enjoying food in its simplest form: throwing a piece of fish on the grill and topping it with a squeeze from a fresh lime, or folding a spoonful of cinnamon whipped cream into a bowl of sliced mangoes. Coconuts, Key limes, pineapples, and bananas all make their way into our repertoire, both at home and at the restaurant. We soak up the flavors of the tropics as much as we do the sunshine.

But every now and then we miss Vermont. We think longingly about the snow and all the fun that comes with it: sledding down the hill in our front yard, shoveling a path to the house after a big storm, and sipping hot cocoa by the fire after a day of skiing. We dream about stews and roasts and ovens filled with cakes and cookies.

Our life is filled with a wide assortment of experiences; that contrast is essential to living what we love. Sometimes we laugh thinking about what appears to be no more than a short attention span. In reality, it's the variety of diverse experiences that makes life come alive.

We love Anguilla and Vermont equally, for different reasons. They feed our souls in different ways, and we've worked hard to make them both important parts of our life. Seasonality has much to do with our schedule, and after about a week in Vermont in January, we're ready to head south again until the fields turn green and the apple trees show the first signs of spring.

# Baked Peaches and Cinnamon Cream

As part of the *Today* show's "Destination Wedding" on the beaches of Anguilla, we were invited to do a cooking segment featuring our favorite tropical recipes. For the show, we made a version of this recipe using mangoes. This one is even better; it tastes like a peach pie without the crust and is far easier to make. Baking peaches intensifies their flavor, and the warm fruit and cool whipped cream melt together perfectly.

PREP TIME: 5 MINUTES
COOKING TIME: 20 TO 30 MINUTES
SERVES 6

6 large ripe peaches
¼ cup sugar
1 cup heavy cream
½ teaspoon ground cinnamon
1 teaspoon pure vanilla extract

Preheat the oven to 400° F. Line a sheet pan with parchment paper.

Cut the peaches in half and remove the pits. Arrange the halves cut side up on the baking sheet and sprinkle with 2 tablespoons of the sugar. Bake for 20 to 30 minutes, or until soft and golden brown.

While the peaches are baking, whip the cream with the remaining 2 tablespoons sugar, the cinnamon, and the vanilla.

Serve the peaches warm, topped with the whipped cream.

# PEACHES AND BISCUITS IN TENNESSEE

Have you ever had a meal at a restaurant so memorable, so perfect in every way, that you can't wait to go back for more? You dream about the flavors, the seductive aromas wafting by your table; you can even picture the waiter who brought you such an unforgettable experience.

Our travels have taken us to magnificent restaurants in France, extravagant banquets in China, and countless other fine dining establishments all over the world. But if you ask what we remember most, which experience we would really love to repeat, one of the first things that comes to mind is breakfast in Nashville, Tennessee.

When given the choice, our family always takes the slow road. We hate to miss anything along the way, and fast food certainly has no character whatsoever. (That's an understatement, isn't it?) One example—as extreme as it may sound—is when we drove our son, Jesse, to college three thousand miles away without getting on a single interstate highway. The trip took three weeks and meals were of great importance. We'd collected an abundance of books and magazine articles about regional foods across the country and tried to savor as many new flavors as we could, as many times a day as possible. Obsessive, perhaps, but it sure is a great (and delicious) way to see America.

Back to breakfast. It was 8:30 and we'd already driven two hours that morning. Heading west out of Nashville, Bob needed coffee and we were all ready for a break. After extensively researching the best place to stop, Jesse and I chose the Loveless Café. The room was small and simple, and tables were covered with red-and-white checkered cloths. We studied the menu briefly and decided to pass on the country ham, grits, and red-eye gravy prominently displayed on the front page. "We'll just have the biscuits and preserves," I said, ordering for the table.

Our waitress arrived fifteen minutes later

using an oven mitt to deliver a black skillet filled with a dozen golden brown biscuits. We smelled them the minute she came through the door and looked at each other, knowing that something great was about to appear on our table. In the other hand she carried a well-worn ceramic bowl filled with an embarrassing mound of peach preserves. For some reason, we'd been expecting three ordinary little biscuits and perhaps a few packages of preserves for each of us. We were so wrong.

If you've never had fresh, hot buttermilk biscuits slathered with homemade peach preserves, you really are missing one of life's greatest pleasures. These particular preserves were out-of-this-world delicious: big pieces of fruit with very little added sugar to take away from their pure, wholesome goodness. The peaches must have been picked at just the right time and they exploded with flavor. We ceremoniously broke open one biscuit after another and watched the peach preserves melt into the warm center of each. After prolonging the experience as long as possible with refills of coffee, preserves, and—yes, even more biscuits—we hit the road and continued our journey.

When we remember Jesse's trip to college, that morning will linger in our minds forever.

# No-Name Dessert

We had a difficult time naming this recipe. In fact, we almost didn't include it because we weren't sure what to call it. It's certainly not a traditional recipe. It has a cake batter, is loaded with fruit like a pie, but is spooned out of the pan like a pudding. We're still not sure what to call it, but the recipe is too good to keep to ourselves.

PREP TIME: 10 MINUTES
COOKING TIME: 20 TO 30 MINUTES
SERVES 4

1 cup all-purpose flour
⅔ cup plus 2 tablespoons granulated sugar
¼ teaspoon salt
1 cup sour cream
1 teaspoon baking soda
4 nectarines, pitted and sliced ¼ inch thick
¾ cup fresh blueberries
1 cup heavy cream
1 teaspoon pure vanilla extract
Confectioners' sugar, for sprinkling

Preheat the oven to 350°F. Butter and flour a 10-inch oval or 6 × 9-inch rectangular baking dish. In a small bowl, whisk together the flour, ⅔ cup granulated sugar, and the salt. Set aside.

In a large bowl, mix the sour cream and baking soda. Add the dry ingredients and mix by hand until just blended. Gently mix in the nectarine slices and blueberries.

Pour the batter into the pan and bake until lightly browned on top, 20 to 30 minutes. When a tester is inserted in the center, it should come out with some moist crumbs still attached.

Whip the cream with the remaining 2 tablespoons granulated sugar and the vanilla. Sprinkle the cake with confectioners' sugar and serve warm, with the whipped cream.

# Key Lime Pie in a Glass

Mention the words "Key lime" and most people will start daydreaming about the sandy beaches of the tropics. Our Vermont home is wonderful because it is close to family and friends, but sometimes we can't help but miss the clear waters of our home in the Caribbean. To cure our blues, we'll often whip up a batch of this fun dessert, look at pictures of our friends in Anguilla, and imagine ourselves back on the beach.

PREP TIME: 15 MINUTES
CHILLING TIME: 4 HOURS
SERVES 4

8 egg yolks
2 (14-ounce) cans sweetened condensed milk
1 cup bottled Key lime juice, well shaken
12 Oreos, finely crushed (see Note)
1 cup heavy cream
2 tablespoons sugar
1 teaspoon pure vanilla extract

In a medium bowl, whisk together the egg yolks with the sweetened condensed milk. Gradually whisk the Key lime juice into the mixture.

Pour about 1 inch of the lime mixture into a clear glass, 3 to 4 inches wide at the top. Sprinkle with a 1/4-inch layer of crumbs. Pour in another layer of Key lime, then more crumbs, and finish with a third layer of Key lime.

Cover with plastic and refrigerate for at least 4 hours, allowing the Key lime mixture to moisten the crumbs.

Whip the cream with the sugar and vanilla. Top each serving with whipped cream and a sprinkle of cookie crumbs.

**NOTE:** The Oreos can be crushed in a food processor or in a plastic bag using a rolling pin.

# Pumpkin Whoopie Pies

Not many foods bring back childhood memories like whoopie pies. This recipe came to us from our friend Jean Temple. After one batch, we were convinced they were even better than the traditional chocolate version. Jean warns—and she is absolutely right—that in order for these to be as rich and moist as possible, it's important to use the entire can of pureed pumpkin, even if it seems like too much at the time.

PREP TIME FOR CAKES: 20 MINUTES
COOKING TIME: 10 TO 12 MINUTES
PREP TIME FOR FILLING: 10 MINUTES
ASSEMBLY TIME: 5 MINUTES
MAKES 2 DOZEN

FOR THE CAKES

3 cups all-purpose flour
1 teaspoon salt
1 teaspoon baking powder
1 teaspoon baking soda
1½ tablespoons ground cinnamon
1½ teaspoons ground cloves
1½ teaspoons ground ginger
1 cup (2 sticks) unsalted butter, at room temperature
2 cups light brown sugar, packed
1 (15-ounce) can unsweetened pumpkin puree
2 large eggs
1 teaspoon pure vanilla extract

FOR THE FILLING

2 egg whites
¼ cup milk
2 teaspoons pure vanilla extract
1 pound confectioners' sugar
1½ cups solid vegetable shortening

Preheat the oven to 350° F. Line two sheet pans with parchment paper.

Make the cakes: In a small bowl, whisk together the flour, salt, baking powder, baking soda, cinnamon, cloves, and ginger.

Using an electric mixer fitted with a paddle attachment, cream the butter and brown sugar on high speed until light and fluffy, 3 to 4 minutes. Add the pumpkin, eggs, and vanilla and beat on medium speed until well blended, scraping down the sides as needed. On low speed, add the dry ingredients and mix until just incorporated.

Place heaping tablespoons of the batter 2 inches apart on the sheet pans. Bake for 10 to 12 minutes, or until the tops spring back when touched. Transfer to a cake rack to cool completely.

Make the filling: Using an electric mixer, beat the egg whites until frothy. On medium speed, add the milk, vanilla, and 2 cups of the confectioners' sugar and beat until blended, 1 to 2 minutes. Add the shortening and remaining 2 cups confectioner's sugar and continue beating until creamy and smooth.

Spread a heaping tablespoon of filling on the flat side of half the cakes and top with the remaining halves.

# Chocolate Croissant Pudding

What do you make when you're being considered to host a television special and you're invited to cook dinner for the president of the network? This was precisely our dilemma when we were negotiating the details of our Fine Living show, *Island Time*. After considering several options, we served this Chocolate Croissant Pudding. It's rich and creamy—and we're pretty sure it's one of the reasons we landed the job.

PREP TIME: 15 MINUTES
COOKING TIME: 45 MINUTES
SERVES 4 TO 6

2¾ cups heavy cream
¼ cup milk
½ cup plus 3 tablespoons sugar
1 cup semisweet chocolate chips
1 large egg
2 teaspoons pure vanilla extract
4 cups (1-inch) cubes of croissants

Preheat the oven to 325° F.

In a medium saucepan, heat 1¾ cups cream, the milk, and ½ cup sugar until the sugar is dissolved; do not allow to boil. Remove from the heat. Add the chocolate chips and whisk until melted.

In a large bowl, whisk together the egg and 1 teaspoon of the vanilla. Gradually whisk in the chocolate mixture until well blended. Cool for 5 minutes, stirring several times.

Add the croissant cubes and stir gently until coated. Transfer the mixture to a 6-cup baking dish and sprinkle the top with 1 tablespoon sugar. Bake for 45 minutes, or until the center of the pudding is just barely set. Do not overbake.

While the pudding is baking, whip the remaining 1 cup cream with the remaining 2 tablespoons sugar and 1 teaspoon vanilla. Serve the pudding warm with the whipped cream.

# S'mores

As children, the best part about summer camp was the s'mores we made almost every night before hitting the sack. Now that we're adults, we carry on the tradition at our campfire circle. Not everyone has a yard that can accommodate a campfire, but if you do, think about finishing up your next barbecue around the fire with this dessert. It's sure to evoke lots of childhood memories.

PREP TIME: 5 MINUTES
COOKING TIME: 5 MINUTES
MAKES 6

6 long forks or sticks, for roasting marshmallows
12 marshmallows
3 plain Hershey bars, broken in half
12 graham crackers

Toast 2 marshmallows over the coals until soft and gooey. Some people will like them golden brown and others crispy and charred. Sandwich the chocolate and melted marshmallows between 2 graham crackers for each serving.

# Chocolate Icebox Cakes with Coffee Cream

We have many fond memories of our old-fashioned icebox cakes covered with whipped cream. The original recipe has appeared for years on the package of Nabisco Famous Chocolate Wafers. Our new improved version uses coffee whipped cream, and these individual cakes produce big smiles every time we serve them.

PREP TIME: 15 MINUTES
CHILLING TIME: 4 TO 6 HOURS
SERVES 4

1 ¼ cups heavy cream
3 tablespoons sugar
1 teaspoon pure vanilla extract
2 teaspoons instant espresso powder
24 Nabisco Famous Chocolate Wafers
1 ounce semisweet chocolate, for garnish

Using an electric mixer, beat the cream, sugar, vanilla, and coffee together until the cream holds its shape.

Spread about 1 tablespoon of the cream onto each wafer. Stack 6 wafers together for each serving, alternating the wafers with the cream and pressing slightly so they hold together. Spread the remaining cream over the outside of the stacks to cover the wafers completely.

Chill for 4 to 6 hours. Grate a sprinkling of chocolate over the cakes and serve.

# Chocolate Chip Oatmeal Cookies

We both have a major sweet tooth. When we bake cookies on snowy Vermont afternoons, it's often difficult to decide what kind to make, since we love them all! This recipe is for all of us who can't make up our minds. It combines chocolate chips with the delicious chewy texture of oatmeal.

PREP TIME: 10 MINUTES
COOKING TIME: 15 MINUTES
MAKES 4 DOZEN

2 cups all-purpose flour
1 teaspoon salt
1 teaspoon baking powder
1 cup (2 sticks) unsalted butter, at room temperature
¾ cup granulated sugar
1 cup light brown sugar, packed
2 large eggs, at room temperature
1 teaspoon pure vanilla extract
2 cups old-fashioned rolled oats
2 cups semisweet chocolate chips

Preheat the oven to 375° F. Line two sheet pans with parchment paper.

In a small bowl, whisk together the flour, salt, and baking powder and set aside.

Using an electric mixer fitted with a paddle attachment, cream the butter and both sugars until light and fluffy. Add the eggs, one at a time, beating well and scraping down the sides of the bowl after each addition. Add the vanilla. With the mixer on low, add the dry ingredients and mix until just incorporated. Add the oats and mix just to blend. Add the chips and mix again briefly.

Spoon heaping tablespoons of dough 2 inches apart onto the sheet pans. Bake until the edges are golden brown, 12 to 15 minutes. Remove from the oven and cool slightly on the pan, then transfer to a wire rack to cool completely.

# Key Lime Pound Cake

There are countless versions of pound cake, but Key lime juice makes this one stand out. It adds the perfect balance of sweet tanginess. Serve it plain for breakfast or brunch, or dress it up for dessert with chocolate sorbet and fresh raspberries.

PREP TIME: 15 MINUTES
COOKING TIME: 45 MINUTES
MAKES 1 LOAF

FOR THE CAKE

1 1/2 cups all-purpose flour
1/4 teaspoon salt
1/4 teaspoon baking powder
1/4 teaspoon baking soda
1/4 teaspoon ground cinnamon
1/2 cup (1 stick) unsalted butter, at room temperature and cut into pieces
1 1/4 cups granulated sugar
2 large eggs, at room temperature
6 tablespoons bottled Key lime juice, well shaken
2 teaspoons pure vanilla extract
1/3 cup plus 1 tablespoon buttermilk

FOR THE GLAZE

1/2 cup confectioners' sugar
2 tablespoons bottled Key lime juice

Preheat the oven to 350° F. Butter and flour an 8 1/2 × 3 1/2 × 2 1/2-inch loaf pan.

Make the cake: In a medium bowl, sift together the flour, salt, baking powder, baking soda, and cinnamon and set aside. Using an electric mixer, cream the butter and 1 cup of the granulated sugar until light and fluffy. Add the eggs one at a time, scraping the sides of the bowl to blend well. Add 2 tablespoons of the Key lime juice and the vanilla, and beat until blended.

On the lowest speed, alternately add the flour mixture and buttermilk. Start with a third of the flour, then add half of the buttermilk, then a third more flour, then the rest of the buttermilk, then the remaining flour. Do not overmix.

Pour the batter into the pan and bake for 45 minutes, or until golden brown and a tester inserted into the center comes out clean.

In a small saucepan, combine the remaining 1/4 cup granulated sugar and 1/4 cup Key lime juice, and cook over medium heat for 2 minutes, or until the sugar is dissolved.

Allow the cake to cool for 10 minutes. Use a knife to loosen the edges, then invert the cake onto a cooling rack. Poke the bottom of the cake at 1-inch intervals with a skewer. Slowly pour the Key lime mixture over the bottom until it is all absorbed.

Make the glaze: Whisk together the confectioners' sugar and Key lime juice in a medium bowl until well blended. Turn the cake right side up and pour the glaze over the top, allowing it to drip down the sides.

# Cooking with Kids

- Parmesan Pita Chips
- Roasted Curried Sweet Potatoes
- Spaghetti and Meatballs
- Nina's Chocolate Chip Kisses
- Orange Berry Ice Cubes
- Chocolate Blueberry Parfaits
- Cinnamon Toast
- Holiday French Toast

# kids in the kitchen

Squeezing a lemon . . . Arranging toppings on a pizza . . . Measuring a spoonful of cinnamon . . . Whisking a salad dressing . . . Breaking an egg . . . Mixing a batter . . . Rolling out dough . . . Assembling a pie crust. With children, any one of these simple tasks can create boundless excitement. The proud look on a child's face after he or she has created a "masterpiece" is unforgettable. They may end up spattered with chocolate and their shirts covered with batter, but chances are they'll have had a great time and even improved their self-esteem along the way.

Plan a cooking project with your kids. Let them read the recipe and figure out what to do. Give them some authority and see how they handle it. You may be very surprised. We can't promise they'll eat everything, but they're more likely to give it a try if they've made it themselves.

Here are a few recipes to get you started. They are written with little hands and young taste buds in mind. Ages and abilities vary, so read the recipes carefully and judge which are most appropriate for your own family. In many cases, the kids will be able to handle most of the preparation and will need your help only when it comes to the stove or the oven.

# Parmesan Pita Chips

These make a delicious snack and are a healthy substitute for potato chips; they're also extremely easy to make. You can break them into small pieces to use as croutons on a salad, as well.

PREP TIME: 10 MINUTES
COOKING TIME: 6 MINUTES
MAKES 32

2 (6-inch) plain pita bread rounds
¼ cup olive oil
½ cup shredded Parmesan cheese

Preheat the oven to 400°F. Line a sheet pan with parchment paper.

Cut the pita bread in half. Cut in half again and then again to make 8 wedges.

Carefully separate the two layers of each piece so you end up with a total of 16 pieces. Arrange the pita wedges rough side up on the sheet pan.

Pour the oil into a small bowl and brush a little onto each pita chip. Using your hands, sprinkle the cheese over the top.

Bake for 5 to 6 minutes, or until golden brown.

# Roasted Curried Sweet Potatoes

Curry might seem an unlikely flavor to serve to children, but when used sparingly, it's usually a great success. Combined here with the natural sweetness of the potatoes, the curry simply adds an interesting yet subtle flavor that will introduce children to something new.

PREP TIME: 15 MINUTES
COOKING TIME: 20 MINUTES
SERVES 6

2 pounds sweet potatoes
6 tablespoons (3⁄4 stick) unsalted butter
1 teaspoon curry powder
1 teaspoon kosher salt

Preheat the oven to 450°F. Line a sheet pan with parchment paper.

Peel the sweet potatoes and cut them into 1-inch chunks.

In a large pot, melt the butter. Add the curry powder and salt, and stir well. Add the potatoes and toss well.

Arrange the potatoes on the sheet pan in a single layer. Roast for 20 minutes or until tender.

# Spaghetti and Meatballs

Shaping the meatballs is a perfect project for kids, and cooking them is so easy since all they have to do is roll them around in the pan until they're done. We'd be hard-pressed to find a more kid-friendly meal from start to finish.

**PREP TIME: 10 MINUTES**
**COOKING TIME: 20 MINUTES**
**SERVES 4**

1 pound ground beef
1 large egg
1/3 cup dried bread crumbs, plain or seasoned (see page 10)
1/4 teaspoon kosher salt
1/4 teaspoon freshly ground black pepper
1 tablespoon olive oil, plus more for tossing
1 pound spaghetti
1 (26-ounce) jar plain marinara or spaghetti sauce
Freshly grated parmesan cheese, for serving

In a large mixing bowl, combine the beef, egg, 1/4 cup water, bread crumbs, salt, and pepper. Using a fork or your hands, mix all the ingredients until they are well blended.

Using your hands, form meatballs about the size of golf balls. You should have about 20 of them.

Heat the tablespoon of oil in a large sauté pan over medium heat until hot but not smoking. Carefully place the meatballs in the pan and cook until cooked through and browned on all sides. Move them around as needed so they cook evenly, about 10 minutes.

While the meatballs are cooking, bring a large pot of lightly salted water to a boil over high heat. Add the spaghetti and cook until tender but still firm. (Tasting is the only way to know for sure.) Drain well in a colander. Return the

spaghetti to the pot and toss with a few tablespoons of olive oil to keep it from sticking together.

Pour the sauce into a large saucepan and bring to a simmer over medium heat. Once it is warm, add the meatballs and stir gently.

Divide the spaghetti among individual bowls. Top with the sauce and meatballs and serve immediately, with Parmesan to be passed at the table.

# Nina's Chocolate Chip Kisses

Cooking can be an adventure for the whole family to experience. Baking with your children is rewarding and fun, giving you an opportunity to pass down family recipes and traditions. These chocolate chip kisses are easy enough for the kids to make, but don't limit yourself to baking them only when they are around! They're just as addictive now as they were when we were ten.

PREP TIME: 12 MINUTES
COOKING TIME: 15 MINUTES
MAKES 4 DOZEN

1 cup sweetened condensed milk
3 cups shredded coconut
1 teaspoon baking powder
2 cups semisweet chocolate chips

Preheat the oven to 325° F. Line two cookie sheets with parchment paper.

In a medium bowl, mix the sweetened condensed milk and coconut. Sprinkle the baking powder over the mixture and blend well. Add the chocolate chips and stir.

Using a teaspoon, drop the mixture onto the prepared cookie sheets in small mounds about 2 inches apart. Bake for 15 to 20 minutes, or until light brown on the edges.

Allow to cool slightly before removing from the pans.

# Orange Berry Ice Cubes

These look particularly pretty in a frosty glass of lemonade. And they're definitely not just for children! We served them at Jesse and Maggie's wedding while guests were waiting for the ceremony to begin.

**PREP TIME: 5 MINUTES**
**FREEZER TIME: 4 HOURS**
**MAKES 16**

1 ¼ cups orange juice
48 raspberries

Pour the orange juice into an ice cube tray. Do not fill it up too much or it will be difficult to carry back to the freezer.

Place 1 or 2 berries in each ice cube section, depending on size. Transfer the tray to the freezer. It will take about 4 hours for the ice cubes to freeze.

Serve the colorful cubes in any cold drink.

# Chocolate Blueberry Parfaits

Part baking and part art, these parfaits are even prettier when served in a glass so you can see all the layers. Kids feel like professional pastry chefs when creating this beautiful dessert.

PREP TIME: 20 MINUTES
SERVES 4

20 Nabisco Famous Chocolate Wafers (see page 10)
1 cup heavy cream
2 tablespoons sugar
½ teaspoon pure vanilla extract
1 cup fresh blueberries

Put the chocolate wafers in a sealable plastic bag, push out all of the air, and seal tightly. Using a rolling pin, crush the wafers to make coarse crumbs.

Using an egg beater or an electric mixer, beat the cream, sugar, and vanilla together until soft peaks form, 2 to 3 minutes. To see if it's ready, turn off the mixer and pull up a small amount of the cream with a spoon. If you can make soft peaks that hold their shape, the whipped cream is ready. Be careful not to overbeat.

Wash the blueberries in a colander under cold water. Throw out any that aren't pretty and blue. Gently pat the berries with a paper towel to dry.

Spoon about 1 tablespoon of whipped cream into each glass. Then sprinkle 1 tablespoon of chocolate crumbs over the cream and top with a layer of blueberries. Repeat the layers three times or more, depending on the size of your glass. Spoon a little whipped cream over the last layer of blueberries.

Garnish with a few berries and serve immediately, or cover the glasses with plastic wrap and refrigerate for up to 6 hours.

# Cinnamon Toast

For us, cinnamon toast brings back wonderful childhood memories of Sunday mornings at the family breakfast table. The cinnamon and sugar melt together with the butter and transform a plain piece of toast into a delicious masterpiece. It's also good made with raisin bread as an after-school snack.

PREP TIME: 5 MINUTES
COOKING TIME: 5 MINUTES
MAKES 4 SLICES

2 tablespoons sugar
2 teaspoons ground cinnamon
4 slices good-quality white bread
2 tablespoons unsalted butter, at room temperature

Mix the sugar and cinnamon in a small bowl.

Place the bread in the toaster and toast until light brown.

Remove the toast and spread some butter on each piece. Using your fingers, sprinkle each slice of toast with the sugar-cinnamon mixture.

# Holiday French Toast

The holidays provide a great opportunity to spend more time with your kids in the kitchen. This season, why not start a tradition by making this French toast with the whole family? Prepared eggnog from the dairy case (without alcohol, of course) is the magic ingredient in this breakfast favorite.

**PREP TIME: 10 MINUTES**
**COOKING TIME: 5 MINUTES**
**MAKES 4 PIECES**

1 cup eggnog
¼ teaspoon ground cinnamon
4 (1-inch-thick) slices white bread or challah
2 tablespoons unsalted butter
1 tablespoon sugar
Real maple syrup, for serving

In a shallow bowl or pie pan, lightly whisk together the eggnog and cinnamon.

Dip the bread slices into the eggnog and let soak for a minute or two on each side. They should be well coated but not soggy.

Heat the butter on a griddle or in a large sauté pan over medium heat. Add the bread and cook until golden brown and cooked through, 2 to 3 minutes on each side.

Sprinkle the toast with the sugar and serve immediately with maple syrup.

**NOTE:** French toast is best when you use bread that's a couple of days old. If it's too fresh, it will become gummy.

# Many Thanks

Before anyone else, we'd like to thank our staff at Blanchard's Restaurant. We love you all: Lowell, Clinton, Miguel, Ozzie, Bug, Tarah, Hughes, Garrilin, Rinso, Alex, Alwyn, Alfonso, Bootsie, and Samaro. You're the best of the best!

We are honored to have worked with a photographer as talented as Ellen Silverman. Thanks, Ellen—we had a great time. Many thanks as well to food stylist Anne Disrude and prop stylist Betty Alfenito, who have a brilliant sense of style and whimsy.

A giant thank-you goes to Annetta Hanna, without whom this book would never have been written. Annetta, we can't imagine writing a book without you.

Many thanks to everyone at Clarkson Potter for their endless enthusiasm and hard work: Natalie Kaire, Pam Krauss, Lauren Shakely, Marysarah Quinn, Maggie Hinders, Philip Patrick, Katherine Dietrich, Alison Forner, Camille Smith, and everyone else behind the scenes.

Michele Parrish and Kristin Dormeyer, what would we have done without you? You saved the day more than once with your magical words. And Patrick and Chad, your remarkable insight helps us clarify our thoughts when we get off track and things get a little fuzzy.

A special thanks goes to Ariana Lewis, Daniel Orem, and Luca Eisen for helping us with the kids chapter. We have to do that again sometime. You were terrific!

Nina Freedman gave us the recipe for the Chocolate Chip Kisses and Jean Temple created the Pumpkin Whoopie Pies. It's great fun to share your goodies with our readers!

To our dear friends Donny French and Becky and Alan Joffrey—without your help we could never do what we do. Thanks for keeping the home fires burning. And to our friends Betsy Siebeck, Gary Smith, Milt and Carolyn Frye, and Susan and Ron Green—thanks for the great night testing S'mores around the campfire.

Thanks to Danny Meyer for your never-ending support and inspiration.
And much appreciation to Barbara Haber for your insight and encouragement.

Many thanks to Jake and Liz Guest and their family, who invited us to spend time at their wonderful Killdeer farm. And to Scott Woolsey, who keeps their farm stand looking picture perfect and always has a taste of something new and delicious to share.

Love to Jesse and Maggie for creating wonderful food memories around the world. Can't wait for our next adventure!

And as always, thanks to all of our friends who share meals with us at home and at the restaurant. Without you, there would be no reason to cook.

# Index